VINTAGE
FURNITURE PAINTING

VINTAGE FURNITURE PAINTING

KAREN PETRUS WILLIAMS

STERLING

New York / London
www.sterlingpublishing.com

PROLIFIC IMPRESSIONS PRODUCTION STAFF:

Editor in Chief: Mickey Baskett
Copy Editor: Ellen Glass
Graphics: Dianne Miller, Karen Turpin
Styling: Lenos Key
Photography: Jerry Mucklow
Administration: Jim Baskett

Library of Congress Cataloging-in-Publication Data

Williams, Karen Petrus.
  Vintage furniture painting / Karen Petrus Williams.
    p. cm.
  Includes index.
  ISBN-13: 978-1-4027-5276-6
  ISBN-10: 1-4027-5276-8
  1. Furniture finishing. 2. Furniture painting. 3. Decoration and ornament--Themes, motives.
  4. Furniture--Repairing. I. Title.

TT199.4.W55 2008
684.1'0443--dc22   2007034326

                    2 4 6 8 10 9 7 5 3 1

Published by Sterling Publishing Co., Inc.
387 Park Avenue South, New York, NY 10016
© 2008 by Prolific Impressions, Inc.
Produced by Prolific Impressions, Inc,
160 South Candler St., Decatur, GA 30030
Distributed in Canada by Sterling Publishing
c/o Canadian Manda Group, 165 Dufferin Street,
Toronto, Ontario, Canada M6K 3H6
Distributed in the United Kingdom by GMC Distribution Services,
Castle Place, 166 High Street, Lewes, East Sussex, England BN7 1XU
Distributed in Australia by Capricorn Link (Australia) Pty. Ltd.
P.O. Box 704, Windsor, NSW 2756, Australia

Printed in China
All rights reserved

ISBN-13: 978-1-4027-5276-6
ISBN-10: 1-4027-5276-8

For information about custom editions, special sales, premium and corporate purchases, please contact Sterling Special Sales Department at 800-805-5489 or specialsales@sterlingpub.com.

About the Artist

Karen Petrus Williams

Karen Petrus Williams began her art career in the 1980's as a graphic artist. She started working at the Palace Department Store in Monroe, Louisiana as a fashion illustrator. Later, when she moved to Shreveport, LA she continued her graphic arts career doing retail newspaper art production. Eventually she became a publicist for Barksdale Air Force Base where she produced brochures, flyers, and posters advertising on-base activities.

In the 90's she decided to switch from the more technical graphic arts field to decorative arts. At this time the hand-painted clothing craze was at its zenith so she took advantage of this trend and opened her first business, "Artisan." She designed art for cloth and employed six artists to paint the designs. These were marketed to retailers throughout the United States and Canada. Six years later, the hand-painted clothing craze faded and furniture became Karen's new canvas. For the past 15 years she has produced hundreds of hand-painted furniture and home decor items for customers across the country. Each year, in April and October, Karen and her husband Joe exhibit and sell at the Roundtop Antique Show in Texas.

When Karen is not painting pieces of furniture for decorators, customer orders, or for her shows, she

Photo of Karen courtesy of Amy Giglio.

and Joe take time to enjoy life on their small farm in north central Louisiana. There they raise miniature donkeys, horses, and cattle. Weekends are spent browsing small-town antique shops and auctions searching for items suitable for very vintage painting.

To see more of Karen's current work, visit her website at www.artisanhandpaintedfurniture.com.

TO JOE.
I love our life together. I thank you for
all your help and encouragement.

Acknowledgements

Many thanks to my children and grandchildren who bring me such pleasure and inspiration. To Angela, Sheri, Marissa, and Vicki – thank you. You all played an important part in helping me make this book a reality. To my parents, Charles and Dollie Petrus – you raised me with an appreciation of all things beautiful, and reverence for God, who created beauty for our pleasure and enjoyment.

CONTENTS

INTRODUCTION

My desire in writing this book is to inspire you, and to teach you the basic painting and preparation techniques that will allow you to design and create your own heirloom furniture and home decor pieces. In the last fifteen years I have experimented and developed a number of shortcuts and tricks of the trade that I want to pass on to you. These techniques will allow you to spend less time preparing the surfaces and more time doing the fun stuff, like painting and designing your own creations.

With my short-cut techniques for painting on antique furniture pieces, there is no stripping of paint or finish. The technique allows the old finish to enhance the painted designs and the painting to become part of the old finish. The look will be vintage – as if it had been painted there for decades.

You'll find instructions and patterns for 20 painted furniture pieces – all with a vintage look. Even though the painting looks like it was always there, the designs are painted afresh on old pieces using acrylic paints. The process I have developed to create this age-old look works on wood, metal, and glass surfaces. Paint manufacturers have developed many new products that allow for better paint adhesion to surfaces.

I am a self-taught artist, so some of my ideas may be contradicted by other artists, but my techniques of building and blending on the surface are easy and pleasing to the eye. I hope you enjoy creating your very own vintage style furniture.

Here is a snapshot of Karen's booth at the Roundtop, TX antique market.

GENERAL SUPPLIES

In this section, you will find information about the paints and brushes used to paint the designs as well as the supplies you will need to clean and prepare different surfaces for painting. Keep these tools and supplies on hand for all the projects. Specific supplies needed for individual projects will be listed with the instructions.

A Word of Caution: Some of the supplies are harsh chemicals and you need to take basic precautions to protect yourself from any harmful effects. Wear chemical-resistant gloves, a long-sleeved shirt, long pants, and eye protection. Always read the manufacturer's instructions and follow them carefully. When using these chemical products, it is always best to work outdoors or in a very well-ventilated area.

Surfaces

Searching for and finding a special treasure to decorate is probably the most enjoyable part of the process. Glass, wood, and metal are all acceptable surfaces. Wood presents a beautiful surface for decoration. Rich grain and warm colors are a perfect background for your art. Flea markets, import stores, antique shops, and even garage sales are just some of the places you may find a wooden piece perfect for decoration.

But don't stop there – metal and glass are great surfaces for vintage painting, too. When their surfaces are prepared properly, you can use your regular acrylic paints and the same blending techniques that work so well on wood.

Look for sturdy items in relatively good condition. Consider the prep time needed to make the item ready for decorative painting. Check for peeling veneer; if it is peeling, can it be glued down or repaired. If not, pass it by – solid wood pieces are much better buys. Look for drawers or doors that open and close easily. Some simple repairs can be made quickly with wood putty and glue, but unless you enjoy repairing furniture choose items that need minimal work.

Before

Preparation Supplies

Preparing Previously Stained and Sealed Wooden Pieces

- **Lacquer thinner** is used to clean and roughen the surface to allow it to take acrylic paint.

- **Steel wool** and **sandpaper** for smoothing rough edges and sanding areas repaired with putty. You will need an assortment of fine to coarse grades of each.

- **Oil based gel stain** is used to coat the entire piece after decoration. This is the secret to the vintage look.

- **Rags, old socks,** for applying the stain to the surface and a small, old **paintbrush** for applying it to trim and crevices.

- **Protective gear:** wear chemical-resistant gloves, eye protection, a long-sleeved shirt, and long pants.

PREPARATION SUPPLIES...CONTINUED

Preparing Unfinished Wood and
Previously Painted Wooden Pieces

- **Pre-stain sealer** for unfinished wood allows the stain to go on more uniformly, especially on soft woods like pine. Use this product only if you plan to stain instead of paint the surface.

- **Liquid sander** for wiping painted pieces you plan to repaint. I prefer the milky type of this product.

- **Primer:** Use this product on unfinished wood only if you plan to base paint the surface with latex paint. Use on painted wood only if you are changing the color significantly. Primer will reduce the number of coats needed to cover the previous paint.

- **Sandpaper:** Have an assortment from coarse, for removing loose paint, to medium and fine grit, for smoothing out rough edges and sanding any puttied areas.

- **Wood putty** and **putty knife** to fill any holes or small cracks in the surface.

- **Latex wall paint** or **bottled acrylic paint** will be your background paint. Use bottled decorative acrylic paints for smaller projects. For larger items, choose latex paint in a quart or gallon quantity. Latex wall paint in semi-gloss or gloss finishes work well for base painting.

- **Paint brushes** and **small roller:** Use a good trim brush for corners, and cover the larger areas with the roller.

Preparing Glass

- **Glass cleaner:** Use blue glass cleaner to clean glass surfaces.
- **Vinegar and water** can also be used to clean glass.
- **Clear polyurethane spray finish:** Use to prepare and seal the surface before painting.

Preparing Tin

- **Lacquer thinner** and **steel wool:** Rub the entire surface with fine steel wool dipped in lacquer thinner to clean and rough up the surface.
- **Spray primer** is used to prime the surface and prepare for the base paint.
- **Spray paint** in flat or gloss finish is used to base paint metal items.
- **Clear polyurethane spray finish** is the final coat that seals and protects your piece.

Base Painting and Finishing Tools

- **Angled trim brush:** Use to base paint the piece with latex paint and to apply polyurethane during the finishing process.
- **Small paint roller:** Use to apply latex paint evenly and smoothly over large areas. Use the foam roller to apply paint and the cloth roller to apply polyurethane.
- **Natural sponge** is needed for the parchment finish described in the "General Information" section.
- **Gel stain** is used to stain over your entire piece after decoration and is the key to the vintage finish. Ask your paint dealer for a high pigment gel stain. Apply with an old sock over rubber gloves.
- **Paint thinner** is used to thin gel stain for lighter application.
- **Waterbase polyurethane,** in a semi-gloss or satin finish, will seal and protect your piece upon completion.

Decorative Paint

I use acrylic paint for the decorative painting because acrylic paint will not dissolve in the oil-based gel stain that gives the vintage look. If you use oil paint for the decorative painting, it will wipe off when you apply the oil-based stain.

Many brands of decorative acrylic paints are readily available. Look for high pigment paints in either bottles or tubes. Choose colors that are pleasing to you and be sure to include White and Black for blending.

All projects are painted wet on wet, which requires blending on the surface. Most projects start with a dark basecoat and lighter colors are painted on top of the wet paint, blending and stroking on the surface. You may need to add **extender** or **blending medium** to your paints to give you more open time for blending. I prefer a watery version rather than a gel. Use a medium from the same manufacturer that is formulated to work with the kind of acrylic paint you are using. If you are working on a dark surface such as stained wood or a black background, you may choose to "paint" the medium on top of the dry base surface between color strokes. Working this way you retain the opaque colors on the dark surface.

I have provided a palette of colors for each project in this book, but don't limit yourself to my choices. The purpose of this book is to show you how to choose and design your projects in the colors you love most.

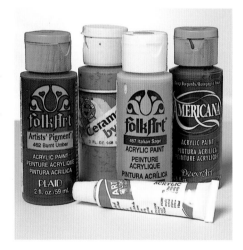

Designing Supplies

Patterns are included for the designs I painted on the furniture pieces. However, you may wish to use parts of one design combined with parts of another design so that it will fit the furniture pieces that you have chosen. Or, you may need to move the design pieces around to make them fit. Or, you may wish to draw your own design – copying a favorite flatware pattern or a motif on a piece of fabric. The following items will be helpful in your design endeavors:

- **Tracing paper** for tracing a design.
- **Transfer paper or graphite paper** for transferring the design to your surface.
- **Fine tip black markers** for tracing over patterns.
- **Pencils** for drawing and marking measurements.
- **Cardstock, poster board,** for making design templates.
- **Scissors and craft knife** for cutting templates
- **Painters tape** for taping designs in place
- **Ruler, triangle, curve templates** and **compass** for measuring and drawing your design.

Brushes

When it comes to brushes, you get what you pay for. Purchase high quality acrylic artist's brushes. Quality brushes produce quality artwork.

Keep your brushes clean. Acrylic paint dries quickly. Clean your brushes thoroughly after use and rinse them with clear water. I have a two-section water basin with a scrubber in the bottom on one side and a clean water well on the other.

Filberts are my favorite brushes. These versatile brushes can be used for numerous applications. On the stroke worksheet, I have specified filberts and rounds for many of the strokes. You must place the filbert flat on the surface and then turn it on its side to achieve many of the strokes. If you have never worked with a filbert in this manner, you may choose to use a round brush for these strokes. The result is very similar, but the petal-shaped edge of the filbert gives the stroke a wonderful, full roundness. Use the stroke worksheets to practice until you decide which brush feels more comfortable to you.

I have specified the brushes and sizes needed for each project. If you are painting the projects in a smaller or larger size, simply use a smaller or larger brush. Keep all your brushes at hand while you paint, and use the brush that best fits the area you are painting and is most comfortable for you.

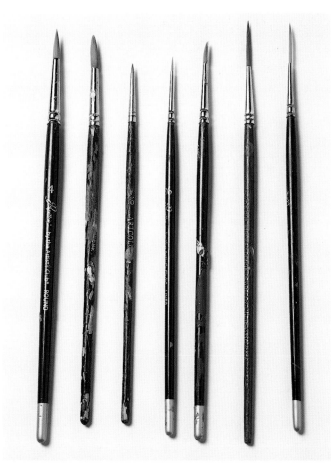

Liners Size 10/0

This brush is used in every project for scrolls, borders, vines, and details. Purchase a good quality, long hair liner.

Rounds Sizes #1, #2, #4

These brushes are used for teardrop strokes, small leaves, and borders.

Flat Sizes #2, #4, ¾", 1"

These brushes are used for borders, basecoating, blending, and shading.

Filbert Sizes #2, #4, #6

This multi-purpose brush is used for all leaves and florals. It can also be used like a round with a slight twist at the end of the stroke to produce a teardrop shape.

Deerfoot & Scruffy

Sizes ⅛", ¼", ½"

Use this brush with extender medium to "mush" wet colors together to produce depth and highlights.

Angle Brush (pictured at left in photo), Sizes ¼", ½", #2

This is the brush to use to paint borders.

Filbert Rake

Sizes ⅛", ¼"

Use this brush for highlighting and finishing details.

GENERAL INFORMATION

In this section you will learn all the tricks for preparing your surfaces and the fundamentals of my decorative painting method. You will find instructions for preparing old and new surfaces for decorative painting. There are also photos that show you how to transfer patterns as well as how to paint roses, leaves, borders, and scrolls.

Preparing Stained and Sealed Wood

When choosing a wooden piece, first check all sides as well as the top for surface damage. If there is veneer damage, consider base painting the item in a solid color, as wood putty can be used to repair some minor flaws when the putty will be covered by paint. You want a piece in good condition with doors and drawers that open easily. Hardware can be removed and replaced. Remember, this is your canvas. You don't want to spend a lot of time on a poor piece that even after decoration will still be only a poor piece.

Most furniture has been stained and sealed with a glossy finish such as lacquer. This surface must be prepared to take acrylic paint.

Before tackling a large, fine piece of furniture try this technique on a small piece that just needs a makeover. You can decide whether you like the finish well enough to do a larger piece. It is quick and easy compared to stripping and sanding but the result may or may not be what you want.

Before

1. **Clean the surface.** Dust with a large, old paint brush, making sure you get in all the cracks and crevices. Turn the piece upside down and remove all dirt, cobwebs, and dust. If needed, use a cloth dampened with mild dishwashing detergent to remove any mud or stubborn dirt. Use a minimal amount of water on your cloth; wood can react badly to too much water. Let the surface dry thoroughly.

2. **Wipe with lacquer thinner.** Work outdoors or in a very well-ventilated area. Wear long pants, a long-sleeved shirt, eye protection, and chemical-resistant gloves. Pour about a cup of lacquer thinner into a metal or glass bowl. Pull an old sock over your glove, dampen it with lacquer thinner, and wipe the entire surface, following the grain where possible. The lacquer thinner degreases and cleans the surface so it will take the acrylic paint. The surface may look a bit uneven because the lacquer thinner softens the original finish. This is normal; after you apply the gel stain and the polyurethane in the finishing process the piece will have a nice, smooth surface.

Note: Occasionally the lacquer thinner may react with the finish to produce white or light-colored streaks or clouds that remain even after the lacquer thinner dries. This is rare, but you should test the lacquer thinner on a small area before wiping the entire piece. If you do get a reaction you may want to paint the item a solid color.

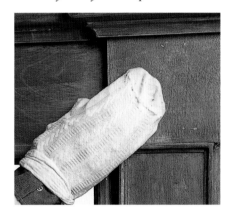

3. **Smooth and remove blemishes with fine steel wool.** After the lacquer thinner dries, look for any areas that are raised, too dark, or too light. Rub with the grain to make the surface more uniform. Remove any drips or spots of paint that may be on the surface.

Always read and follow label directions when using any chemical solvents.

Preparing Unfinished Wood

A smooth surface is the most important factor whether you plan to stain or paint. If needed, sand the piece to remove rough edges. Fill nail and staple holes with wood putty, let dry, and sand smooth.

If you plan to stain the piece, this is done after the decorative painting. Use an electric palm sander to remove as much of the putty as possible. If the piece is pine, apply a pre-stain solution before painting the design. Pine is a soft wood and takes stain differently from most other woods. Someone at your local paint store can help you select a product that will help your stain go on more evenly. After decorative painting, your piece is ready for staining.

If you plan to paint the piece, prime it first. You can spray, brush, or roll the primer on. Your paint store can tint primers for you. Use a latex dark gray or red oxide primer if you plan to paint the piece a dark color. If you plan to paint in pastels or lighter colors, use white latex primer. Apply the primer everywhere you plan to apply paint. After the primer dries, sand any areas that appear rough. Apply a semi-gloss or satin latex wall paint in the color of your choice. Let the paint dry, and it is ready for your decoration.

Preparing Painted Wood

Have you ever spotted a great piece of furniture at a garage sale – perfect size, perfect height – but it's purple! Don't pass it by. Paint can make it any color you like, and your decorative painting will transform it into a treasured heirloom.

1. **Hardware:** If the hardware has been painted, you may decide to leave it on and paint over it. If not, or if you plan to replace the hardware, remove it. If there are indentions left by the original hardware, fill with wood putty then sand if necessary.
2. **Clean and remove any loose paint from the surface.** Scrape away loose paint with a paint scraper, being careful not to take off more paint than you intended and damage the wood underneath. Don't forget the inside of doors or drawers and shelves. If the inside of your project is in good condition you may choose to clean it well and paint only the outside.
3. **Sand** with medium grit sandpaper.
4. **Fill in any cracks or holes with wood putty,** using a putty knife to apply and wipe away any excess. Sand the puttied surface after it has completely dried.
5. **Apply liquid sander.** I prefer the type that is a milky liquid. Suit up and put on your chemical-resistant gloves. An old sock over your glove will make a great applicator and will not fall off. Wipe a thin coat over the entire surface. Let it dry 15 to 30 minutes depending on the humidity. When the surface has dried to a tacky feel, it is ready for paint or primer.
6. **To prime or not to prime – that is the question.** If you are painting a piece in the same hue as the original color [dark, medium, or light hues] there is no need to prime, but if you are going to take it to a much lighter or much darker color, priming will result in fewer coats and less work for you.

    Use a piece that was painted purple as an example. If you plan to paint this piece darker, there is no need to prime. If you plan to paint it white, you need to prime with a latex white or light gray primer. If the old piece was white and I wanted to paint it black, I would use a red oxide or dark gray primer.

7. **Base paint** with a good latex semi-gloss or satin wall paint. Use a good 1" angle brush for corners and trim areas, working the paint into all the areas that a roller or paint pad will not reach. Cover the rest of the piece with a roller or paint pad; use a brush if you prefer. Following the paint manufacturer's instructions, let the first coat dry and apply another if necessary.

    You can base paint small projects such as boxes, step stools, or wooden trays with small bottles of decorative acrylic paint. These small bottles are inexpensive and available in any color. Be sure to purchase enough bottles to cover your project.

Preparing Glass

Old, wood-framed glass windows are wonderful items to decorate. Look for sturdy windows.

1. If the window is very dirty, clean it outdoors with a water hose and dishwashing liquid.
2. Remove any paint from the glass surface with a flat edge blade while the window is wet. (Paint comes off more easily when the glass is wet.) Let it dry and caulk any loose panes. Clean the glass again with window cleaner or vinegar and water.
3. Most old windows are painted white. You may choose to just clean them well and leave the weathered frame as is. If you choose to paint the window frame, do it now.
4. Prepare the glass for painting. I paint on glass with regular acrylics. The techniques taught in this book require blending on the surface. To prepare the glass surface to accept the paint, spray it lightly with clear polyurethane. This gives the surface tooth; the paint will adhere to the surface of the spray. The spray will give the window a clouded look but it is still quite pleasing.
5. After you complete your decorative painting, spray again with the same clear polyurethane, sandwiching the paint between the two coats. Don't bother to tape off the wooden areas when spraying the glass; the entire window will be coated with clear polyurethane in the finishing steps.

Preparing Metal

Metal surfaces such as tin and silver plate are among my favorites. The texture takes the paint well and makes blending colors a delight. Rusty tin is a wonderful surface to paint. The brush glides smoothly over the old surface.

If your surface is enameled metal or silver plate:

1. The surface will be very slick and must be roughed up a bit. Dip a fine steel wood pad in a little lacquer thinner and rub the entire item. This will remove any surface dirt and roughen the surface to accept the next step.
2. After drying, spray the entire item with an aerosol primer for metal surfaces. Let dry.
3. Spray with the base color of your choice, using aerosol paint. The surface is now ready for your decorative painting.

To prepare rusted tin:

1. Gently rub the surface with fine steel wool to remove any loose rust.
2. *You may spray the surface with paint, but chances are some of the old rust will eventually show through; this may be a pleasing look.* My favorite look is to paint directly on the rusty tin, stain it, and seal it with a clear spray. The result will be a dark reddish brown background with an aged appeal.

Transferring Designs

With Transfer Paper

You will need to enlarge the patterns in this book in order to use them for the large pieces of furniture shown. Your local print shop or blue print shop can do this for you. If you have a printer/scanner setup with your computer, you can copy the patterns on the scanner and use your print program to enlarge it. There is also a setting for a mirror image. The enlargements will probably be printed on "tiles" – sections of the pattern printed out on 8½" x 11" regular copy paper that you will tape together to assemble the large patterns.

Because the patterns are so large and no two pieces of furniture are the same, we have given the patterns to you in pieces. This will make it easier for you to adjust and customize the patterns to your particular piece of furniture. Use the photos as a guide for placing the designs and feel free to tailor them to your piece. Most times, it is best to transfer only the larger elements, do not attempt to transfer every line. For example, transfer only a circle shape or a general outline for the roses so that you can fill in with the proper strokes. Lines for the vines should not be transferred, they can be free-hand painted and added at will to fill in areas and balance your design.

1. **Trace** your patterns with a fine tip black marker on tracing paper. The black marker provides an image you can see through the back of the tracing paper. You will use the original tracing and this "back side" image on many of the projects that require a mirror image.

2. **Transfer** your pattern to your painting surface. Tape the traced pattern down on two sides. Slide a piece of transfer paper underneath. Use a hard lead pencil, ballpoint pen, or stylus to trace the pattern onto your surface.
   I prefer yellow or white transfer paper. I always mark a big "X" on the side that should be up. There's nothing sadder than tracing an entire project only to find your transfer sheet was upside down. (See Photo 1.)

Mirror Image Patterns: If the design is repeated as a mirror image, simply flip the pattern over to the other side and transfer it to the surface. (See Photo 2.)

If you are copying and enlarging the design you can place the traced pattern upside down on the copier. The copier will print the image it "sees" through the tracing paper. The image will be a bit lighter but will produce the mirrored design you need. If the copier has a mirror image setting (for printing an iron-on transfer, for example) you can have the copier print the mirror image for you.

One-, Two-, and Three-Part Patterns: Some of the projects require multiple patterns. Transfer and paint the first pattern, let the paint dry, and transfer the next pattern on top of the dried paint. Follow the instructions provided with each project.

Using Templates to Transfer Designs

Templates are outlines of your design motifs (containers, fruits, ovals, or florals) cut from cardstock. You can add and remove items and move them around until you achieve a design that pleases you, and you can use them again and again for different projects. For a mirrored pattern, just flip them over.

1. To make a template, trace the outline of your art onto tracing paper.
2. Transfer it to cardstock or poster board.
3. Cut it out.
4. Here's an easy way to create a template for a symmetrical item such as a flowerpot. Draw a center line down a piece of cardstock. Draw (or transfer) half of the item on one side of the line. Fold the cardstock along the center line. Cut out with scissors, following the outline of your half shape. Unfold the cardstock and you have a perfectly symmetrical item.
5. Tape the templates in place on your surface to create the desired design. (See Photo 3.)
6. Trace around the templates to transfer the outline of the designs to the surface. (See Photo 4.)

Try using a combination of templates and transferred patterns together to create your own masterpiece.

Photo 1. Transferring a design with transfer paper.

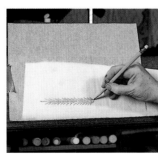

Photo 2. Flipping the traced pattern over to make a mirror image.

Photo 3. Taping templates in place.

Photo 4. Tracing around templates.

Adding Edging and Borders

I like to use square paint pads as an applicator to quickly add borders or edging to a furniture piece. Paint pads are foam and fabric paint applicators, available in most hardware stores. A 2" pad is available with a handle. For borders, simply cut the refill pads to the size you need.

1. Cut the plastic slide off the back of the paint pad refill.

2. Measure the size you need and mark it on the back. Cut along the line. Bend the cut strip in half to use as a handle.

3. Notice the finger placement. Use your pinky to steady the stroke and your index finger to apply pressure to the pad.

4. Use the edge, trim, or lip of the piece as a guide. Pull the pad downward to paint the border.

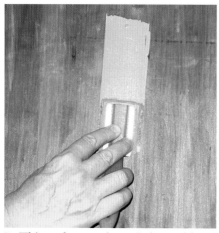

5. This pad comes in a 2" size and has a plastic handle. It is perfect for applying wider borders.

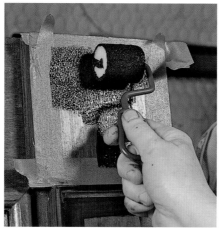

6. Tape off a regular geometric shape, such as a square or rectangle. Apply paint with a roller or brush. When you remove the tape, the shape will have straight edges.

Squares were made by taping off. Edging done with a paint pad. See page 121 for photo of project.

Distressing & Staining

Distressing and staining give a warm, vintage look to your project. This is always done after you have done the decorative painted design on the surface.

Photo 1. This photo shows the painted piece before distressing. Finished project is pictured on page 106.

Photo 4. Use a small brush to apply gel stain in crevices.

Photo 5. Wipe away the stain with a clean rag.

Photo 2. Lightly sand the edges and raised areas. Dust well.

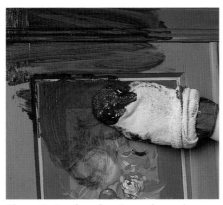

Photo 3. Apply gel stain to the entire surface, wiping it on with a rag or an old sock over your glove.

Photo 6. Continue wiping until you have achieved the look you desire. Let dry and finish with a coat of clear polyurethane.

Parchment Finish

A parchment finish is easier and quicker than base painting. If the piece is painted a solid color and is in relatively good shape, you can lighten or darken the shade with glaze and paint. You can also use this technique to disguise a poor paint job or add texture to a dull piece. I have used this method to take a white piece down to a cream finish or take a blue piece to a light, muted blue. On the dark side I have used dark red or dark brown over black to create a deep, rich surface. It is best to use light paint over light surfaces and dark paint over dark surfaces.

Supplies:

Acrylic paint (or latex)
Faux finishing medium
Sea sponge
Container for mixing paint
Mixing stick

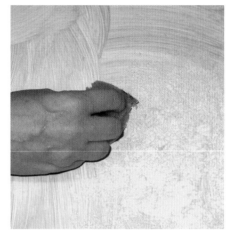

How to:

1. Mix one part acrylic faux finishing medium with one part paint.
2. Apply this paint to the surface using either an old sock or a large natural sponge. Wipe this paint mixture over the entire piece as if you were washing it; be sure to cover all surfaces.
3. Using an artist's sponge or a natural sea sponge, tap the sponge lightly over the wet area. When the sponge becomes full, squeeze out the excess paint. Continue tapping the surface. The result will be a parchment look.

Design Painting Technique

All of the projects in this book are painted wet in wet. You begin by painting a dark base color to establish the shape of a flower, leaf, or fruit, then you add lighter colors on top of the wet paint, blending as you stroke. Depending on the speed of your painting and the humidity in your area, you may need to add extender medium to give you more open time to paint.

Painting Scrollwork

Scrolls add elegance to your vintage painted pieces. They can be intertwined with vines, leaves, flowers, and fruits or provide a border or a corner accent.

Begin by painting the flowing lines of the transferred pattern with a liner brush. Add rounded tips to the lines with a filbert or a round brush. Continue to embellish the scroll with C-strokes, leaves, and curved, elongated teardrop shapes made with a filbert or round brush.

Photo 1. Move your whole arm, not your hand alone, to create smooth, flowing curves with a 10/0 liner brush.

Photo 2. Paint teardrop shapes on the tips of the scroll lines with a filbert or a round brush, pulling toward the scroll line.

Painting a Leaf

1. **First Layer of Strokes.** Using a filbert brush, basecoat the leaf with a dark green. Start at the bottom of the leaf, pulling strokes from the outside edge in toward the leaf center. Continue upward, shortening the strokes as you approach the tip of the leaf.

2. **Second Layer of Strokes:** Follow the original strokes with a lighter green, pulling only halfway to the leaf center.

3. **Highlight Strokes:** Use a filbert rake brush to add White strokes, pulling from the edges toward the center of the leaf. Vary the lengths of the strokes.

4. **Add Tint:** Use a filbert rake brush to add touches of color from surrounding florals or fruits.

5. **Rake Edges:** Use a filbert rake brush and White to highlight the leaf and define the edges.

Painting a C-Stroke Rose

1. Using a filbert brush and C-strokes, basecoat the rose in a dark solid shade.

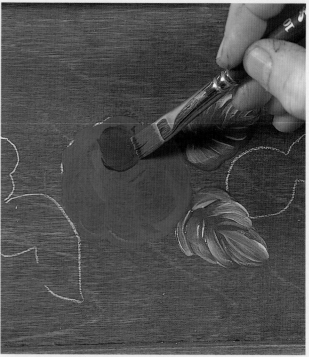

2. Dip your filbert brush in a dot of Black and mix with the basecoat color. Add the darker center to the rose.

3. Mix the basecoat color with White. With the filbert brush, paint a U shape around the dark center to form the cup of the rose.

4. Continuing to use the filbert brush and the lighter mix, make C-stroke petals around the edges of the rose.

5. Add petal strokes around the cup of the rose.

6. Continue adding rows of petals with the filbert brush.

7. Using the filbert brush and White, highlight the petals by painting over the edges of the original strokes.

Designing for Furniture Styles

This section will show you some additional ideas for decorating furniture. I have a note-book full of sketches that I refer to when starting a new project. Trace over some of the furniture patterns here and begin sketching your own ideas. This will be a valuable tool for designing your own pieces.

Round table or tray

Oval table or tray

Two-door cabinet with panels painted on

Two-door armoire with drawer florals and borders

*Two-door nightstand using oval silhouette
and scroll pattern*

*Swag borders and roses
Edge border adds elegance*

*Buffet painted with fruits and florals
Swag greenery mimics oval silhouette*

*Panels are silhouettes painted on flat doors.
Scrolls add interest.*

*Oval wreaths and rope borders
simple & elegant*

Floral designs using mirrored patterns

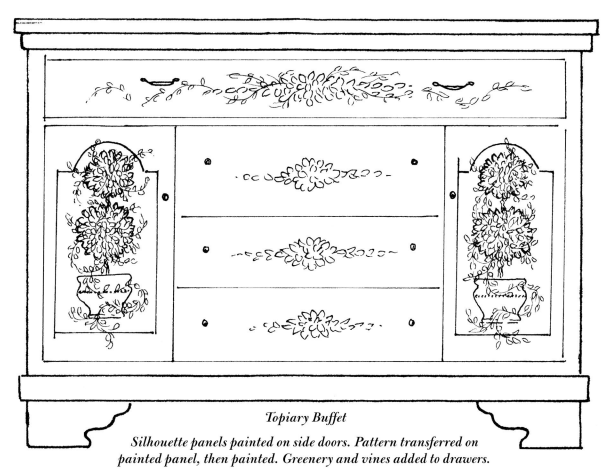

Topiary Buffet

Silhouette panels painted on side doors. Pattern transferred on painted panel, then painted. Greenery and vines added to drawers.

Interesting shaped panels are painted on, then florals are added.

Scroll designs mirrored on each drawer.

Strokes #1 Painting Worksheet

#2 Filbert Teardrop

#4 Filbert Teardrop

#4 Filbert C-stroke
Practice stroking from both directions

#2 Filbert

#2 Filbert

#4 Filbert S-stroke   Side by side for rope border.

#2 Filbert   Practice long to short.

#2 Round   Practice in different sizes.

#4 Filbert   Practice C-stroke for rose design.

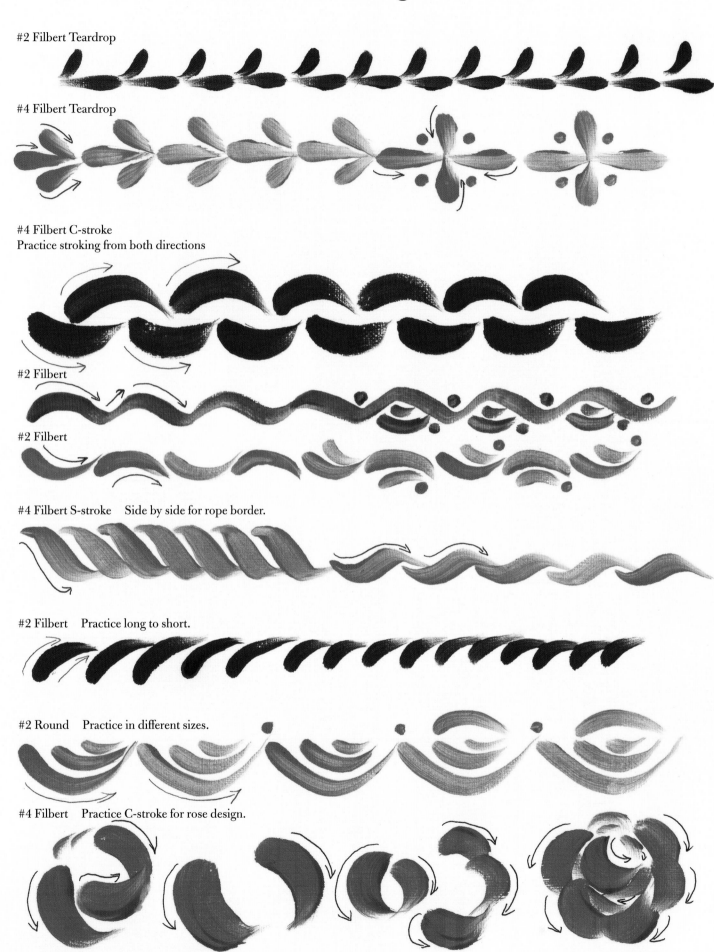

Strokes #2 Painting Worksheet

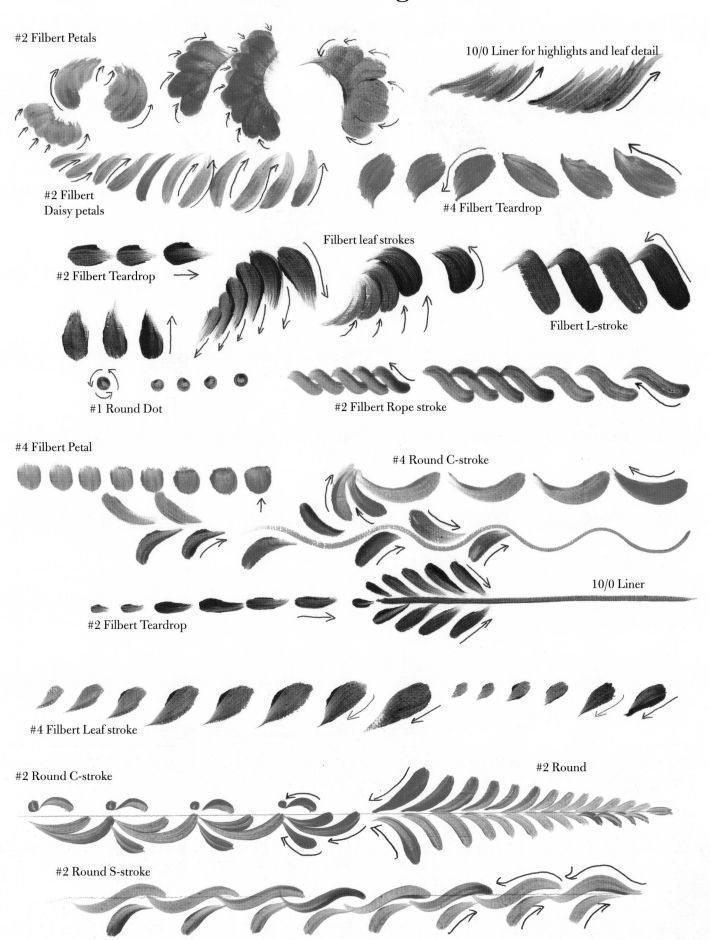

#2 Filbert Petals

10/0 Liner for highlights and leaf detail

#2 Filbert
Daisy petals

#4 Filbert Teardrop

#2 Filbert Teardrop

Filbert leaf strokes

Filbert L-stroke

#1 Round Dot

#2 Filbert Rope stroke

#4 Filbert Petal

#4 Round C-stroke

10/0 Liner

#2 Filbert Teardrop

#4 Filbert Leaf stroke

#2 Round C-stroke

#2 Round

#2 Round S-stroke

Scrolls Painting Worksheet

Scroll I

1. Paint over the transferred pattern with the 10/0 liner and Golden Brown.

2. With the #2 round and Honey Brown, make a teardrop stroke on the tip of the line, pulling toward the line.

3. Continue with the #2 round, adding C-stroke embellishments to the scroll with Honey Brown and Golden Brown.

4. Continue with the #2 round and Honey Brown, making teardrop strokes for center embellishments.

Honey Brown

Golden Brown

Scroll II

1. Paint over the transferred pattern with the 10/0 liner and Honey Brown.

3. Add highlights with the #2 round and Golden Brown.

2. Add tips with the #2 round and Honey Brown.

4. Continue to add highlights with the #2 round and Golden Brown to the C-strokes and teardrop strokes.

Scrolls Painting Worksheet

Burnt Sienna

Camel

Scroll III
Corner Scrolls

1. Paint over the transferred pattern with the 10/0 liner and Camel.

3. Add highlights to scroll tips with the #2 round and Camel. For more emphasis, add White to the tips, following the original stroke with a #1 round.

2. Add tips to scroll ends with the #2 round and Burnt Sienna, using teardrop strokes and C-strokes.

2. With a #2 round and Celery, paint small teardrop strokes on one side of the scroll line.

3. Repeat with Pine Green on the other side of the scroll line.

Scroll IV
1. Paint and highlight the scrollwork first.

4. Add a longer leaf to the inner tips of the scroll with Pine Green.

5. Highlight the Pine Green teardrop leaves with Celery, using the #1 round and following the original strokes.

6. You may wish to add flowing vines and leaves to finish your project. *Refer to the Leaves & Vines Painting Worksheet.*

Leaves Painting Worksheet

Hauser Green Dark   Olive Green   Celery   Golden Brown   Camel   White

Use the wet on wet technique unless otherwise specified. If needed, add extender medium to give you more open time to paint.

PULL IN LEAF

1. Use a #4 filbert and Hauser Green Dark. Starting at the bottom outside and pulling to the center, make strokes progressively shorter to tip. Repeat on the opposite side.

2. Follow the original strokes with the #4 filbert and Olive Green. Pull strokes from the outside halfway in to the center on both sides of the leaf.

3. With the #4 filbert and Celery, follow the original strokes, making them shorter than the Olive Green strokes.

4. Follow the original strokes to highlight the leaf, using the ¼" filbert rake and White, pulling toward the center. Add color to the leaf edges with the filbert rake, using Golden Brown and Camel, or colors from fruits and flowers.

PULL OUT LEAF

1. Use a #4 filbert and Hauser Green Dark. Starting at the bottom, pull gently curved strokes out from the center, making strokes progressively smaller until you reach the tip of the leaf. Repeat on the opposite side of the leaf.

2. With a #2 filbert and Olive Green, follow the original strokes with shorter strokes as shown.

3. Continue with the #2 filbert and Celery, following the original strokes with strokes in varying lengths.

4. Highlight with the ⅛" filbert rake and White. Add touches of White, Camel, and Golden Brown on leaf edges with the filbert rake.

LONG LEAF

1. Basecoat with a #4 round and Olive Green. Start at the bottom and pull strokes upward.

2. With a #2 round and Hauser Green Dark, make a line up the center of the leaf. Add upward strokes as shown.

3. With the 10/0 liner and Celery, refine the veins, following the original stroke pattern.

4. Use the ⅛" filbert rake to add random touches of White and Golden Brown, following the leaf veins and previous strokes.

Leaves & Vines Painting Worksheet

Twisted Leaf
This is a Pull Out Leaf with a little twist at the top.

Use the wet on wet technique unless otherwise specified. If needed, add extender medium to give you more open time to paint.

1

2

Paint this leaf following the instructions for the Pull Out Leaf. Add a one-sided, smaller leaf at the top as shown, resulting in a twisted look.

Vines & Leaves
Move your arm, not your hand alone, to make these loose, wavy lines for your vines.
- Thin the paint to an inky consistency with extender medium.
- Following the transferred design, paint vines with the 10/0 liner and Olive Green.

Leaf Fern
1. Make a long arched line with a 10/0 liner and Golden Brown.
   Add teardrop stroke leaves with a #4 round and Golden Brown, shortening the leaf strokes as you go up the stem.

2. Use the ¼" filbert rake to add highlights with Camel, then White.

- Use a #2 filbert or a #2 round to make teardrop strokes, adding leaves to the vine. Make leaves larger at the base of the vine and smaller as you move toward the tip of the vine.
- Continue adding leaves, changing the color to Celery. Using two or three colors for leaves adds interest and depth.

2. Use the 10/0 liner and Hauser Green Dark to add details to the leaves and stem.

Long Leaf Fern
1. Paint the stem with the 10/0 liner and Celery.

Using a #2 filbert and Celery, pull strokes toward the stem, starting at the bottom with long strokes and shortening the strokes as you go up the stem.

C-Stroke Rose Painting Worksheet

Use the wet on wet technique unless otherwise specified. If needed, add extender medium to give you more open time to paint.

1. Basecoat the rose with Burgundy C-strokes.

2. Add Pink C-strokes to form the cup of the rose.

Use a #4 filbert brush to paint the rose.

Burgundy

Pink

Gold

White

3. Continue with Pink C-strokes to make petals.

4. Highlight the rose with White, following the previous strokes.

5. When the paint is dry, add more White highlights to the edges of the petals. Tap Gold in the center of the rose.

Use shorter Pink strokes to emphasize the cup area.

Note: Paint the leaves first and let them dry before you begin painting the rose.

Add vines and small leaves to finish. Accent some of the leaves with colors from the rose.

When painting smaller or larger roses, use a smaller or larger filbert brush.

Filbert Rose Painting Worksheet

Use the wet on wet technique unless otherwise specified. If needed, add extender medium to give you more open time to paint.

1. Basecoat the rose using a #6 filbert and Barn Red, using C-strokes and working left to right in a circle.

Barn Red   Peach   White

2. With the #6 filbert and Peach, follow the Barn Red strokes, pulling halfway in toward the center.

3. With the #6 filbert and Peach, add the center row of petals. Follow the contour of the rose.

   Brush the entire rose with a light coat of extender medium if the paint is dry.

4. Add shorter strokes to the center cup and center top of the rose.

5. To highlight, use a #4 filbert and White to make short, light strokes on the edges of the petals, following the direction of previous strokes.

Add leaves and vines if desired.

When painting smaller or larger roses, use a smaller or larger filbert brush.

Bud Rose & Filler Flowers Painting Worksheet

Use the wet on wet technique unless otherwise specified. If needed, add extender medium to give you more open time to paint.

Bud Center Rose

White   Baby Pink   Peony Pink   True Red

1. Using a #4 round, paint in True Red and Peony Pink as shown.

2. With a #2 filbert and Baby Pink, add lighter petals, stroking downward toward the center bottom of the rose.

3. Let dry. Paint the entire rose with a thin coat of extender medium. Use a #2 filbert and White to add short, small C-strokes to the inside top of the cup.

4. Use the #2 filbert and White to add white tips to the edges of the petals, following the original strokes and the contour of the rose.

Filler Flowers

White   Camel   Golden Brown   Baby Blue   True Blue

Basecoat the blue flower with the #2 filbert and True Blue.

With the #2 filbert and Baby Blue, add petals to the blue flower with short teardrop strokes.

With the #2 filbert and White, highlight petals randomly on the blue flower. Add the center to the gold flower with the #2 filbert and Golden Brown.

With the #2 filbert and White, add highlights to petal edges.

Use a #1 round to dot the center with White and Golden Brown.

Add a little Black to Golden Brown and dot around the center with a #1 round, as shown.

1. Using the #2 filbert and Golden Brown, make two C-strokes facing each other to form each petal of the gold flower.

2. With the #2 filbert and Camel, add strokes following the original strokes of the gold flower petals, but shorter.

3.

Geranium Painting Worksheet

Use the wet on wet technique unless otherwise specified. If needed, add extender medium to give you more open time to paint.

Deep Burgundy True Red Baby Pink White Pine Green Leaf Green

1.

Finish painting the leaves and let them dry before painting the flowers.

With a #6 filbert and Pine Green, pull inward with facing C-strokes to form leaves.

2.

Highlight leaves with a #2 filbert and Leaf Green.

Use a #4 filbert and Baby Pink to add the petals forming the flower clusters.

Petals:
With a # 4 filbert, make teardrop strokes with Deep Burgundy and True Red as shown. Pull strokes toward the center, using Deep Burgundy at the bottom and True Red at the top of the flower cluster.

3.

Highlight leaves with the #2 filbert and White.

Define and highlight geranium petals with the #2 filbert and White as shown.

Add vines and leaves if desired.

Hydrangea Painting Worksheet

Use the wet on wet technique unless otherwise specified. If needed, add extender medium to give you more open time to paint.

True Blue Royal Purple Baby Blue Honey Brown White

2. With a #4 filbert and Baby Blue, add petals, creating the flower clusters.

1. With a #4 filbert, basecoat with True Blue and Royal Purple. Working wet in wet, brush Royal Purple at the bottom of the ball shapes and True Blue at the top.

4. Continue with the #2 filbert, adding more White to petals to highlight the ball shape.

Use a #2 round and Honey Brown to dot flower centers and highlight leaves if desired.

3. With a #2 filbert and White, define petals and form individual flowers.

Add vines and leaves if desired.

Daisy Painting Worksheet

Use the wet on wet technique unless otherwise specified. If needed, add extender medium to give you more open time to paint.

Antique Gold Camel White Pine Green Celery Burnt Sienna

Burnt Orange

With a #4 flat and Antique Gold, make a round or oval shape for the daisy center.

With the #2 filbert and Golden Brown, pull long petal strokes from the outside in toward the center.

With the #2 filbert and Camel, add shorter petal strokes to the daisy.

With the #2 filbert and Camel, make a second row of inner petals.

With the #2 filbert and White, add tips to petals with short strokes pulling from the outside.
Indicate a second and third row of petals as shown.

Use the tip of a #1 round to add dots to the centers as shown, using Burnt Sienna, Pine Green, Celery, and Burnt Orange.

41

Urn Painting Worksheet

Use the wet on wet technique unless otherwise specified. If needed, add extender medium to give you more open time to paint.

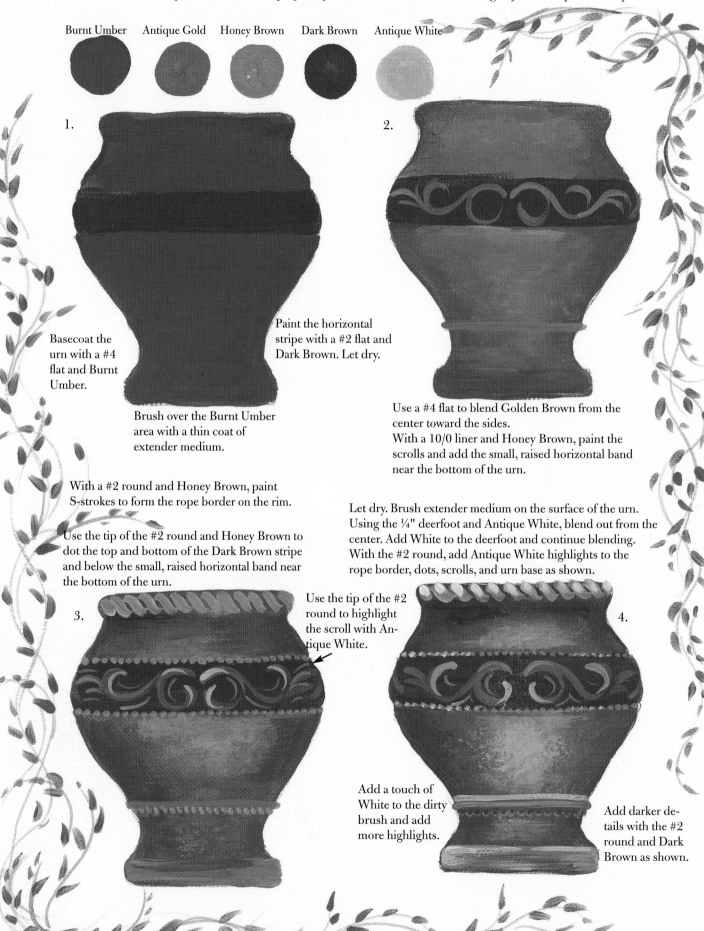

Burnt Umber   Antique Gold   Honey Brown   Dark Brown   Antique White

1.

2.

Basecoat the urn with a #4 flat and Burnt Umber.

Brush over the Burnt Umber area with a thin coat of extender medium.

Paint the horizontal stripe with a #2 flat and Dark Brown. Let dry.

Use a #4 flat to blend Golden Brown from the center toward the sides.
With a 10/0 liner and Honey Brown, paint the scrolls and add the small, raised horizontal band near the bottom of the urn.

With a #2 round and Honey Brown, paint S-strokes to form the rope border on the rim.

Use the tip of the #2 round and Honey Brown to dot the top and bottom of the Dark Brown stripe and below the small, raised horizontal band near the bottom of the urn.

Let dry. Brush extender medium on the surface of the urn. Using the ¼" deerfoot and Antique White, blend out from the center. Add White to the deerfoot and continue blending. With the #2 round, add Antique White highlights to the rope border, dots, scrolls, and urn base as shown.

3.

Use the tip of the #2 round to highlight the scroll with Antique White.

4.

Add a touch of White to the dirty brush and add more highlights.

Add darker details with the #2 round and Dark Brown as shown.

Flower Pots Painting Worksheet

Use the wet on wet technique unless otherwise specified. If needed, add extender medium to give you more open time to paint.

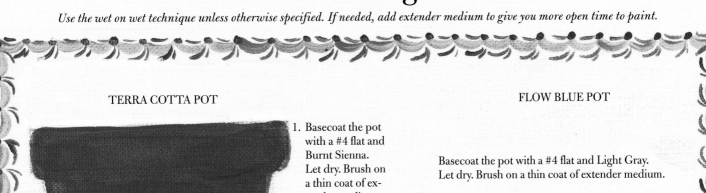

TERRA COTTA POT

1. Basecoat the pot with a #4 flat and Burnt Sienna. Let dry. Brush on a thin coat of extender medium.

2. Add a touch of Black to Burnt Sienna. Use a #2 flat to shade under the lip of the pot and above the saucer. Blend horizontally.

   With a #2 flat, add Golden Brown and blend strokes on the lip, the saucer, and the body of the pot.

3. Using a ¼" deerfoot and Camel, dab and blend outward. Add Antique White and continue dabbing and blending.

   Stroke horizontally with the #2 flat and White to add highlights.

Burnt Sienna	Golden Brown	Camel	Antique White	White

Black

FLOW BLUE POT

Basecoat the pot with a #4 flat and Light Gray. Let dry. Brush on a thin coat of extender medium.

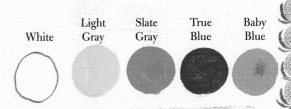

White	Light Gray	Slate Gray	True Blue	Baby Blue

1. Use a #2 flat and Slate Gray to shade the sides, pulling down. Continue toward the center of the pot, blending as you go.

2. Paint the bud stems and the horizontal line at the bottom of the pot with the 10/0 liner and True Blue. Paint the buds, petals, and teardrop stroke leaves with a #2 round and True Blue.

3. Use the #2 round and Baby Blue, following the original strokes to highlight the bud, petals, and leaves. Let dry.

To highlight, brush vertically down the center of the pot with the ¼" filbert rake and White mixed with extender medium. Add a few shorter highlight strokes toward the edges, as shown.

Aster & Tulip Painting Worksheet

Use the wet on wet technique unless otherwise specified. If needed, add extender medium to give you more open time to paint.

Aster

1.

Antique White

Pine Green

Celery

White

Paint the stems with a 10/0 liner and Pine Green.

With a #4 filbert and Antique White, add a center bud to each stem. Make buds larger at the bottom and smaller as they approach the tip of the stem.

With a #2 filbert and Antique White, add a petal to each side of the buds on the larger bottom flowers.

2.

With a #2 filbert and White, add highlights, following the original bud and petal strokes.

3.

Use a #2 round and Pine Green to add a teardrop stroke at the bottom of each bud, pulling toward the stem.

Highlight the stem with a 10/0 liner and Celery.

4.

Use a #2 filbert to dab a bit of Celery on top of the Pine Green at the base of each bud.

Add leaves if desired.

Antique White

Barn Red

White

Pine Green

Open Tulip

1.

With a #2 filbert and Antique White, paint four strokes to form each petal, pulling the strokes down toward the stem.

Paint the stem with a 10/0 liner and Pine Green.

Following the stroke direction, make shorter strokes with a 10/0 liner and White to highlight and define the petal edges.

Add the flower base at the top of the stem with a #1 round and Pine Green.

3.

2. With a ⅛" filbert rake and Barn Red, pull down from the top of each petal toward the bottom center of the tulip.

2.

After the gel stain is applied, the flower will have a warm, antique hue, muting the bright colors. This gives the painting its vintage look.

4.

44

Apple Painting Worksheet

Use the wet on wet technique unless otherwise specified. If needed, add extender medium to give you more open time to paint.

1. Basecoat the apple with a #4 flat and Burgundy. With a ¼" filbert rake and Brilliant Red, add rounded strokes following the apple contours. Let dry. Paint the apple with a thin coat of extender medium.

1.

Burgundy   Brilliant Red   Antique Gold   White

With a #4 flat and Antique Gold, make a C-stroke at the top of the apple.

Immediately begin pulling the Antique Gold down from the C-stroke with a ¼" filbert rake.

2.

With a #4 flat and White, make another C-stroke at the top of the apple.

3.

Immediately use the ¼" filbert rake to pull the White down in varying stroke lengths, following the original contour strokes.

4.

Add a stem, leaves, and vines, if desired.

Pears & Plums Painting Worksheet

Use the wet on wet technique unless otherwise specified. If needed, add extender medium to give you more open time to paint.

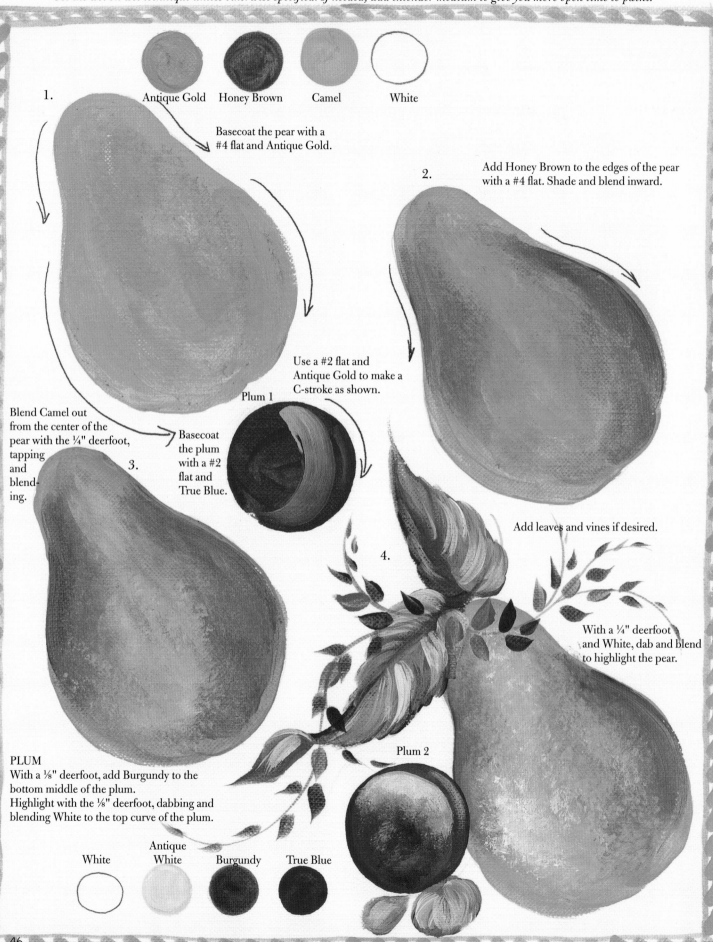

Antique Gold   Honey Brown   Camel   White

1.

Basecoat the pear with a #4 flat and Antique Gold.

2.

Add Honey Brown to the edges of the pear with a #4 flat. Shade and blend inward.

Use a #2 flat and Antique Gold to make a C-stroke as shown.

Plum 1

Blend Camel out from the center of the pear with the ¼" deerfoot, tapping and blending.

3.

Basecoat the plum with a #2 flat and True Blue.

4.

Add leaves and vines if desired.

With a ¼" deerfoot and White, dab and blend to highlight the pear.

Plum 2

PLUM
With a ⅛" deerfoot, add Burgundy to the bottom middle of the plum.
Highlight with the ⅛" deerfoot, dabbing and blending White to the top curve of the plum.

White   Antique White   Burgundy   True Blue

Borders Painting Worksheet

1. Cut a paint pad for black stripe. Use #4 filbert and Black to make half dots. S-strokes with a #4 filbert and Gold. Dots and dash with #2 round and Antique White. Add a short Antique White teardrop stroke "toe" to the bottom of the S-stroke.

Borders are just a series of strokes combined to make a frame for your art. Use the strokes you have learned to make up your own border designs. Paint borders in the predominant colors of your artwork.

2. With a #2 filbert and Antique White, paint teardrops first, then dots.

3. With a 10/0 liner and Celery, make a wavy line. Add C-strokes inside waves, each smaller than the one before.

4. With a #2 filbert and Antique White, make slightly overlapping S-strokes to form the rope.

5. With a 10/0 liner and Pine Green, make a wavy line. With a #2 filbert and Pine Green, add teardrop strokes for leaves. Turn the filbert upon its edge to form the leaf tip.

6. With a 10/0 liner and Antique White, paint a straight center line. With a #2 round and Antique White, pull in teardrop strokes from each side, then add teardrop strokes down the center.

7. With a 10/0 liner and Pine Green, paint a straight center line. With a #2 filbert and Pine Green, pull out teardrop strokes to make leaves on each side of the line, larger to smaller. Add dots with a #1 round and Celery.

8. With a #4 filbert and Pine Green, make large C-strokes. With a #2 filbert and Pine Green, add progressively smaller teardrop strokes below the C-strokes. With a #2 round or #2 filbert and White, add C-strokes, then teardrop strokes above the original C-strokes to finish.

9. Paint an oval with a #4 flat and Black. Add C-strokes with a #2 filbert and Black. Add C-strokes with Antique White above the black C-strokes. With a #2 filbert and Black, add C-strokes, then teardrops, then dots on the outmost layer. With a #2 round and Antique White, add dots on the oval and small C-strokes above the Black dots on the outmost layer.

PAINTED PIECES

The art, photos and instructions in this chapter are designed to inspire you and teach you to create your own vintage furniture. The sample artwork shown on the instruction pages will appear brighter than the art on the finished pieces because they show the decorative painting before adding antiquing gel.

Here are some tips:

• Unless otherwise indicated, the painting processes shown in this book require you to start with the darker colors and add and blend the lighter colors on top, using a wet on wet technique.

• You may need to add extender medium to your acrylic paints to allow more open time for blending.

• You will also notice I use white highlights on every project. When the gel stain is applied in the finishing process the tone and hue of the artwork will be toned down considerably. You must paint "bright" so your work will not be "lost" when the stain is applied.

• Remember to refer to the painting worksheets for additional instructions on painting specific parts of each project.

• Use the palette of colors given for your chosen project if it is different from that of the worksheet.

Pictured on opposite page: Topiary Armoire, see page 50 for instructions.

Dark random leaves radiate from the center.

Add lighter colored leaves.

Add vines and smaller leaves.

TOPIARY ARMOIRE

This elegant topiary design enhances any room. Not too feminine, not too masculine, it exudes classic charm and subtle colors that complement many decors. This design is easily modified by adding florals, changing the shape of the greenery, or using a different container.

SUPPLIES

- Acrylic paints *(See Palette of Colors)*
- Extender medium
- Brushes
  Liner – 10/0
  Filbert – #2, #4, #6
  Filbert Rake – ⅛", ¼"
  Flat – #2, #4, 1"
  Round – #2
  Deerfoot – ¼"
- Armoire or tall, two-door cabinet
- Walnut gel stain
- Waterbase polyurethane
- Tools & supplies for preparing, transferring, antiquing, and finishing

PREPARATION

This was an older piece with minor flaws and damage. The finish was worn and there were a few small scratches.

1. Prepare furniture piece for painting. See "Preparing Stained and Sealed Wood" in the General Information chapter.
2. With pencil draw ovals on door for the leaf border.
3. Enlarge pattern for urn on a copier. Trace and transfer the design to the doors.
4. Using a compass draw the three circles for the topiary, each spaced 2" apart to allow for trunk between them. It is best to free-hand paint the vines and trunks rather than transfer them.

PALETTE OF COLORS

Burnt Umber

Hauser Green Dark   Olive Green   Celery   Dark Brown

Honey Brown   Antique Gold   Antique White   White

Olive Green and Celery.

Vines:

Follow the instructions on the Leaves & Vines Painting Worksheet, but change the palette.

1. Paint the vines with Celery.
2. Add smaller leaves with Hauser Green Dark, Olive Green, and Celery.

FINISHING

1. Wipe the entire surface of the piece with gel stain.
2. After a few minutes, wipe off the gel stain. Be sure to wipe with the grain of the wood. Use a small, old brush to smooth away any gel stain that has pooled in crevices or carved areas. Let dry.
3. Finish with two coats of water base polyurethane applied with a small cloth roller. Use a brush for detail areas. Let dry between coats. ❧

Pattern

Enlarge Pattern for urn to 200% for actual size.

Combine parts A & B
to complete pattern

Part A

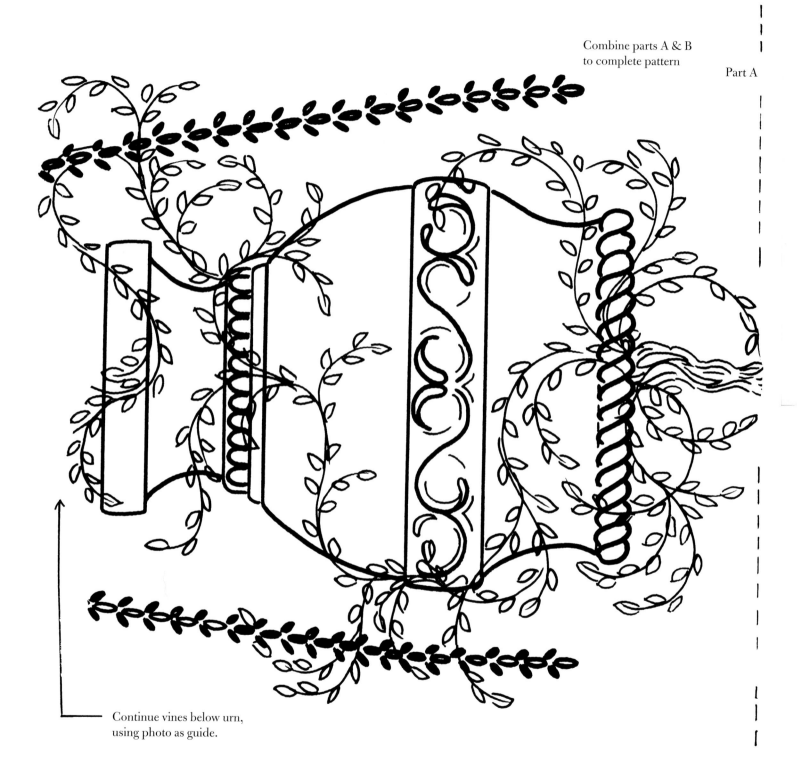

Continue vines below urn,
using photo as guide.

Part B – Bottom circle

Add 2 additional circles for topiary
Bottom circle = 9"Top circle = 7"
Center circle = 8"

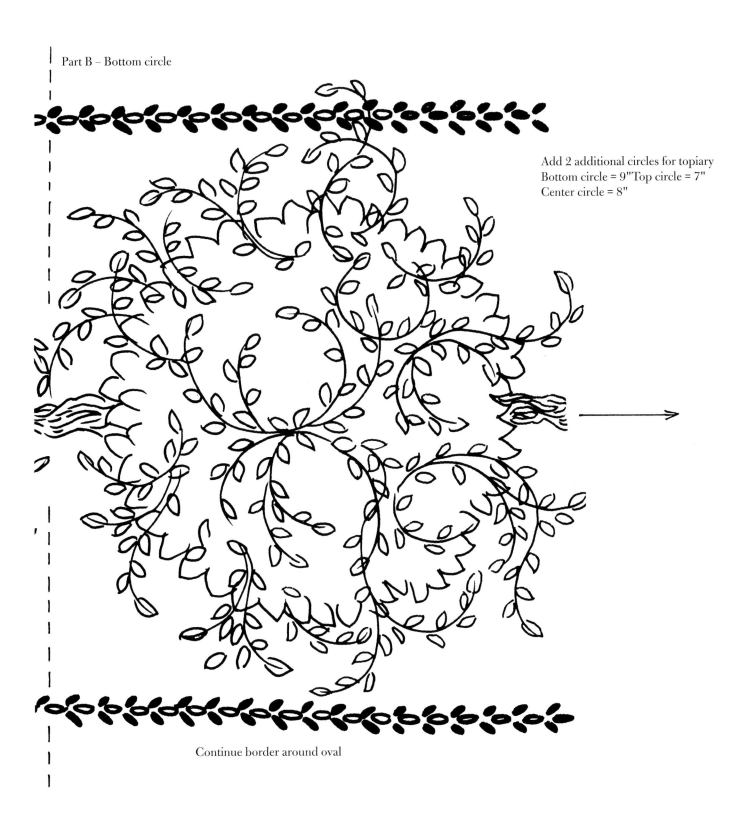

Continue border around oval

PANELS OF ROSES TRUNK

This romantic design can transform an old wooden box into an elegant heirloom trunk. It is a perfect addition at the foot of a bed, as a coffee table, or by the back door for storage. You could easily substitute color combinations from your existing decor for the color palette shown here.

SUPPLIES

- Acrylic paints *(See Palette of Colors)*
- Extender medium
- Brushes:
    Liner – 10/0
    Filbert – #2, #4
    Filbert Rake – ⅛", ¼"
    Flat – 1", #2
    Round – #2
- Wooden box or trunk
- 1" paint pad
- Walnut gel stain
- Waterbase polyurethane
- Tools & supplies for preparing, transferring, antiquing, and finishing

PALETTE OF COLORS

Honey Brown	Camel	Dark Brown	Barn Red	Hauser Green Dark	Olive Green	White

Transfer and paint the panels first. Add the border with Honey Brown, using the 10/0 liner and #2 flat.

Transfer and paint the scrolls.

Transfer and paint the florals and greenery last.

PREPARATION

This was an older piece with minor flaws and damage. The finish was worn and there were a few small scratches.

1. Prepare furniture piece for painting. See "Preparing Stained and Sealed Wood" in the General Information chapter.
2. Trace and enlarge the patterns. Transfer the patterns as needed. The panels then the scroll overlay patterns will be transferred and painted first. After they are dry, then transfer the rose patterns to the panels.

PAINT THE DESIGN

Panels:

1. Transfer the patterns for the solid panels on the top and front of the box. For the top, use the panel shape for the front, just elongate it to fit the top of your trunk.
2. Paint the panels with the 1" flat brush using Camel. Let dry.
3. Line the edges of the panels using the 10/0 liner and Honey Brown.
4. Using the #2 flat brush and Honey Brown, add short square strokes to the inside of the border. Let dry.

Scrolls:

Refer to the Scrolls Painting Worksheet.

1. Transfer the patterns for the scrolls to the top and front panels. Flip the front panel pattern for the second half of the scroll. Repeat for second panel on front. For the top, the scroll will also need to be flipped to create a mirror image for the second half of the scroll.

2. Paint the scroll lines on the panels with Honey Brown using the 10/0 liner.
3. Add the rounded tips to the scroll lines on the panels with Camel using the #2 filbert for the smaller scrolls and the #4 filbert for the larger ones on the top.
4. Transfer the patterns for the leaves, florals, and vines. Flip the front panel pattern and transfer a mirrored image to the other front panel.

Leaves Around Florals:

Refer to the Leaves Painting Worksheet.

1. Basecoat the leaves with the #4 filbert and Hauser Green Dark.
2. Stroke with Olive Green.
3. Highlight with a filbert rake and Camel. Let dry.

Large Roses:

Follow the instructions on the Filbert Rose Painting Worksheet, but use the #4 filbert and change the palette.

1. Basecoat the large roses with the #4 filbert and Barn Red.
2. Stroke the cup and petals with a mixture of Barn Red + White.
3. Highlight with White.

Small Roses:

Follow the instructions on the C-Stroke Rose Painting Worksheet, but use the #2 filbert and change the palette.

1. Basecoat the smaller roses with the #2 filbert and Dark Brown.
2. Stroke the cup and petals with Camel.
3. Highlight with White and a touch of White + Barn Red.

Filler Flowers:

Follow the instructions on the Bud Center Rose & Filler Flowers Painting Worksheet, but change the palette.

1. Basecoat the filler flowers with Dark Brown.
2. Paint the teardrop-stroke flower petals with Camel.
3. Highlight with White and a touch of White + Barn Red.

Vines:

Follow the instructions on the Leaves & Vines Painting Worksheet, but change the palette.

1. Paint the vines with Olive Green using the 10/0 liner.
2. Add smaller leaves with Hauser Green Dark and Olive Green using the #2 filbert.

Highlights:

Add White highlights to the florals and leaves with the ⅛" filbert rake.

Edging & Borders:

Refer to the Borders Painting Worksheet.

1. With the 1" paint pad, edge the top and sides of the box with Honey Brown.
2. Referring to Border #7, add fern-like detail borders on the top and sides. Paint the leaves with Olive Green and the berries with Camel. Let dry.

FINISHING

1. Wipe the entire surface of the trunk with gel stain.
2. After a few minutes, wipe off the gel stain. Be sure to wipe with the grain of the wood. Use a small, old brush to smooth away any gel stain that has pooled in crevices or carved areas. Let dry.
3. Finish with two coats of water base polyurethane applied with a small cloth roller. Use a brush for detail areas. Let dry between coats. ❦

Patterns

Repeat this section

Rose panel for top
Enlarge at 200% for actual size

Extend lines at right to
match left side.

Continue border
around edge of
panel.

Border above
front panels

Scroll Overlay for Top
(actual size)
Repeat as mirror image on
opposite end of panel.

Vertical Leaf Border
(actual size)

Front Panel
Enlarge at 200% for actual size

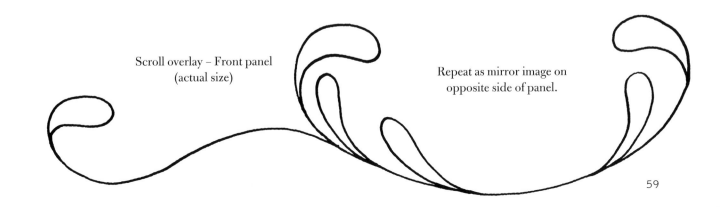

Scroll overlay – Front panel
(actual size)

Repeat as mirror image on
opposite side of panel.

VINING ROSES ARMOIRE

This light and airy armoire would be a charming addition to any room. Shown here on a stained wood surface, the pattern would be beautiful painted on a solid color background. This design could also be painted on a flat-front chest of drawers to match the armoire. Just use the part of the pattern that is the height of your furniture.

Finish with vines and small leaves

Add White to highlight.

Add lighter colors and White to highlight florals.

Basecoat leaves and roses with their darkest tones.

SUPPLIES

- Acrylic paints *(See Palette of Colors)*
- Extender medium
- Brushes
  Liner – 10/0
  Filbert – #2, #4, #6
  Filbert Rake – ⅛", ¼"
  Round – #2
- Armoire or tall, two-door cabinet
- ½" paint pad
- Walnut gel stain
- Waterbase polyurethane
- Tools & supplies for preparing, transferring, antiquing, and finishing

PREPARATION

This was an older piece with minor flaws and damage. The finish was worn and there were a few small scratches.

1. Prepare furniture piece for painting. See "Preparing Stained and Sealed Wood" in the General Information chapter.
2. Enlarge, trace and transfer the design on the first door. Flip the pattern over, trace and transfer a mirrored image on the second door.
3. Use pieces of the pattern to customize a pattern for the bottom horizontal design.

PAINT THE DESIGN

Border:

With the paint pad and Antique Gold, edge all the way around both doors and drawers as shown. Let dry.

Scrolls:

Refer to the Scrolls Painting Worksheet.

1. Paint the scroll lines with Honey Brown using the 10/0 liner.

Continued on page 62

PALETTE OF COLORS

Pine Green   Celery   Honey Brown   Antique Gold   Antique White

Deep Burgundy   White   Barn Red

. . CONTINUED

2. Add the rounded tips to the scroll lines with Antique Gold. Let dry.

3. Following the instructions for Scroll IV, paint the leaves on the scrolls with Pine Green and Celery. Let dry.

Leaves Around Florals:

Refer to the Leaves Painting Worksheet.

1. Basecoat the leaves with the #4 filbert and Pine Green.

2. Stroke with Celery, then Antique Gold.

3. Highlight with a filbert rake and White. Let dry.

Roses:

Follow the instructions on the C-Stroke Rose Painting Worksheet, but change the palette.

1. Basecoat the roses with Deep Burgundy.

2. Define the petals and cup of the rose with a mixture of Deep Burgundy + White.

3. Highlight with White.

Tulips & Asters:

Follow the instructions on the Aster & Open Tulip Painting Worksheet.

Vines:

Follow the instructions on the Leaves & Vines Painting Worksheet, but change the palette.

1. Paint the vines with Celery.

2. Add smaller leaves with Pine Green and Celery.

FINISHING

1. Wipe the entire surface of the armoire with gel stain.

2. After a few minutes, wipe off the gel stain. Be sure to wipe with the grain of the wood. Use a small, old brush to smooth away any gel stain that has pooled in crevices or carved areas. Let dry.

3. Finish with two coats of water base polyurethane applied with a small cloth roller. Use a brush for detail areas. Let dry between coats. 🌱

Patterns

Vining Roses Armoire – Pattern
Enlarge @250% for actual size

Top – Part A

Bottom – Part B
Connect at dotted lines
co complete pattern.

PALETTE OF COLORS

Honey Brown   Camel   Antique White

Black

Transfer and paint the Black areas first, then transfer the scroll patterns.

10/0 liner

Add scroll ends with the #2 filbert or #2 round.

Add highlights to scrolls.

CLASSIC SCROLLS HALF-ROUND TABLE

This elegant table is a great project for beginners who are ready to try their hand at scrollwork. Black and gold make a wonderful color combination, but don't limit yourself! The decorator colors popular now would be perfect for this project. A round table would also work well for this project – just double the design.

SUPPLIES

- Acrylic paints *(See Palette of Colors)*
- Extender medium
- Brushes
  Liner – 10/0
  Filbert – #2, #6
  Flat – 1"
  Round – #2
- Half round or half moon table
- Walnut gel stain
- Waterbase polyurethane
- Tools & supplies for preparing, transferring, antiquing, and finishing

PREPARATION

This table is a new reproduction piece. The surface has a slick, lacquered finish. We plan to re-stain the entire table but we still must apply the lacquer thinner so the acrylic decorative paint will adhere to the surface.

1. Prepare furniture piece for painting. See "Preparing Stained and Sealed Wood" in the General Information chapter.
2. The area on the top, inside the scroll border is solid black; and the areas inside the scrolls on the legs are solid black. Enlarge and trace the patterns. Transfer the outline for the solid black areas. Do not transfer the pattern for the scrolls until the black areas have been painted and dry.

PAINT THE DESIGN

Solid Black Areas:
Paint all the solid black areas on the top and legs of the table first, using a #6 filbert and Black. Let dry.

Scrolls:
Refer to the Scrolls Painting Worksheet.

1. Trace and transfer the scroll patterns.
2. Paint the scroll lines with Honey Brown.
3. Add the rounded tips and C-strokes with Camel.
4. Highlight with Antique White.

FINISHING

1. Wipe the entire surface of the piece with gel stain.
2. After a few minutes, wipe off the gel stain. Be sure to wipe with the grain of the wood. Use a small, old brush to smooth away any gel stain that has pooled in crevices or carved areas. Let dry.
3. Finish with two coats of water base polyurethane applied with a small cloth roller. Use a brush for detail areas. Let dry between coats. ♛

Closeup of Top

Closeup of Front

Patterns

Classic Scrolls Half-Round Table Patterns
Enlarge @ 175% for actual size.

Table Legs

(Black Area)

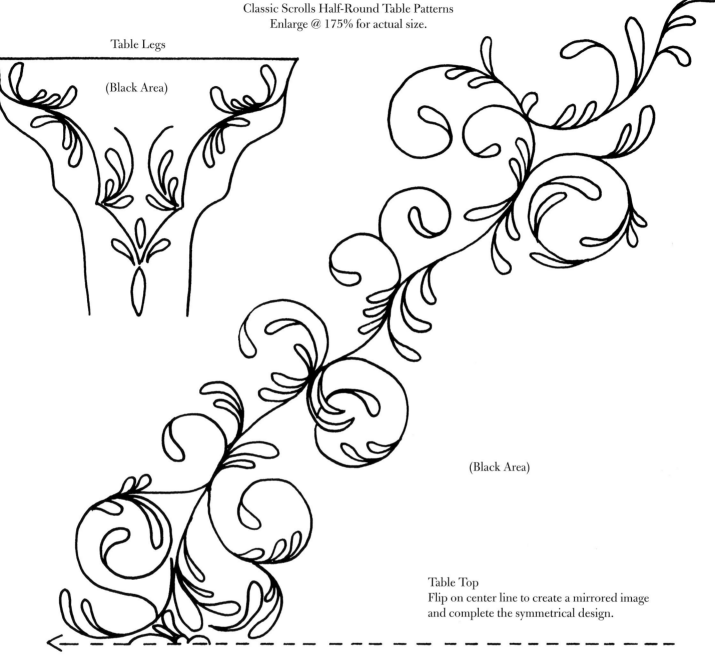

(Black Area)

Table Top
Flip on center line to create a mirrored image
and complete the symmetrical design.

Front – Lip

Repeat around front

Reverse & repeat (mirror image) on opposite side of center.

SUPPLIES

- Acrylic paints *(See Palette of Colors)*
- Extender medium
- Brushes
  - Liner – 10/0
  - Filbert – #2, #4, #6
  - Filbert Rake – ⅛", ¼"
  - Flat – 1"
  - Round – #1, #2, #4
- Rectangular desk or table
- 1" paint pad
- Walnut gel stain
- Waterbase polyurethane
- Tools & supplies for preparing, transferring, antiquing, and finishing

PREPARATION

This was an older piece with minor flaws and damage. The finish was worn and there were a few small scratches.

1. Prepare furniture piece for painting. See "Preparing Stained and Sealed Wood" in the General Information chapter.
2. Trace the patterns.

PAINT THE DESIGN

Black Oval, Border & Legs:

1. Transfer the solid black area of the cameo design.
2. Paint the oval with a 1" flat and Black.
3. Paint the 1" border around the desk top, the apron and the front of the legs with the 1" paint pad. Let dry.
4. Transfer the roses pattern to the black cameo area.

Borders:

Refer to the Borders Painting Worksheet.

1. Paint the border around the edge of the black cameo following the instructions for Border #9.
2. Paint the border around the desk top edge, following the instructions for Border #1.

Continued on page 70

OVAL CAMEO DESK

The wide, detailed borders on this piece appear challenging at first glance, but they are made with combinations of simple brush strokes. This impressive desk is sure to become a vintage treasure.

Leaves Around Florals:

Refer to the Leaves Painting Worksheet.

1. Basecoat the leaves with the #4 filbert and Burnt Umber.
2. Using the #4 filbert, stroke with Honey Brown, then Camel.
3. Highlight with a filbert rake and White. Let dry.

Filler Flowers:

Refer to the Bud Rose & Filler Flowers Painting Worksheet.

1. Basecoat with Dark Brown.
2. Add petals with Honey Brown, then Golden Brown and Camel.
3. Highlight with White.
4. Dot centers in small flowers with the #1 round and Black.

Small Roses:

Follow the instructions on the C-Stroke Rose Painting Worksheet, but change the palette.

1. Basecoat the smaller roses with Burnt Umber.
2. Define the petals and cup of the rose with Camel.
3. Highlight with White.

Large Roses:

Follow the instructions on the Filbert Rose Painting Worksheet, but change the palette.

1. Basecoat the large roses with Dark Brown.
2. Define the petals and cup of the rose with Honey Brown, then Camel.
3. Highlight with White.

Vines:

Follow the instructions on the Leaves & Vines Painting Worksheet, but change the palette.

1. Paint the vines with Camel.
2. Add smaller leaves with Camel and Golden Brown.

FINISHING

1. Wipe the entire surface of the desk with gel stain.
2. After a few minutes, wipe off the gel stain. Be sure to wipe with the grain of the wood. Use a small, old brush to smooth away any gel stain that has pooled in crevices or carved areas. Let dry.
3. Finish with two coats of water base polyurethane applied with a small cloth roller. Use a brush for detail areas. Let dry between coats. ❦

Add lighter colors and White.

Transfer and paint Black areas first, then transfer floral patterns.

Basecoat leaves with darkest tone.

PALETTE OF COLORS

Camel

White

Black

Golden Brown

Burnt Umber

Honey Brown

Dark Brown

Pattern

Enlarge at 180% for actual size.

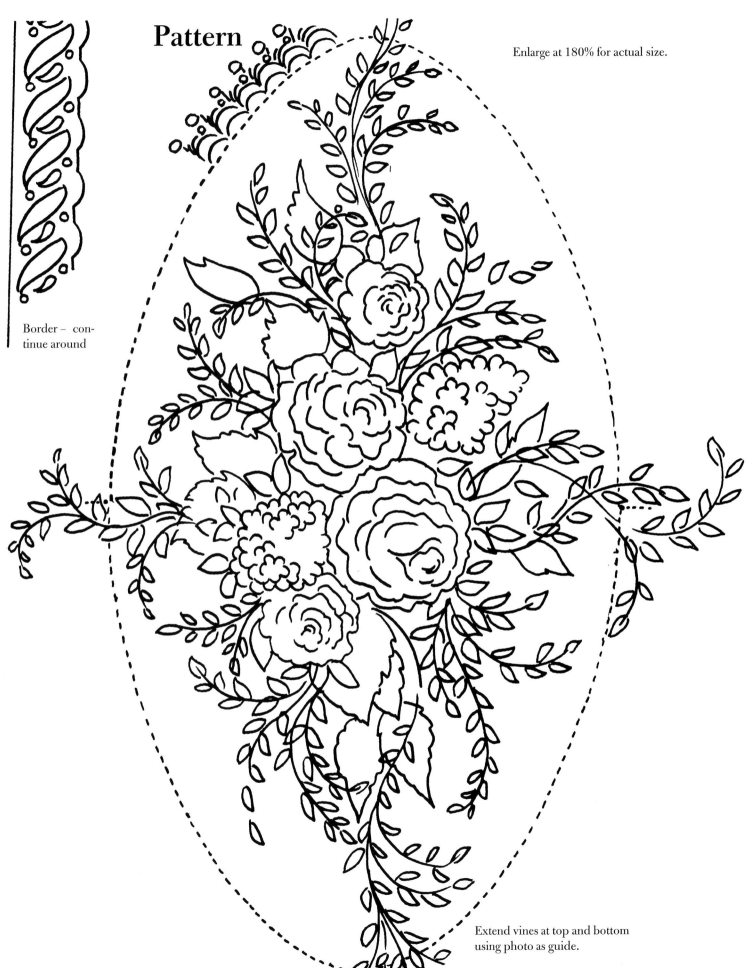

Border – continue around

Extend vines at top and bottom using photo as guide.

DELLA ROBBIA TRUNK

Paint around the design panels on this trunk, leaving the wood as the background for a lovely fruit and floral design. Black was used on this trunk, but for a brighter result you might try cream, mustard, or olive green as an alternative.

SUPPLIES

- Acrylic paints *(See Palette of Colors)*
- Extender medium
- Brushes
    Liner – 10/0
    Filbert – #2, #4, #6
    Filbert Rake – ⅛", ¼"
    Flat – #4, 1"
    Round – #1, #2
    Deerfoot – ¼"
- Trunk, wooden box, or cedar chest
- Walnut gel stain
- Waterbase polyurethane
- Tools & supplies for preparing, transferring, antiquing, and finishing

PREPARATION

This was an older piece with minor flaws and damage. The finish was worn and there were a few small scratches.

1. Prepare furniture piece for painting. See "Preparing Stained and Sealed Wood" in the General Information chapter.
2. Using a pencil and ruler, draw rectangular panels where the design will be painted.
3. Enlarge and trace the patterns. Transfer the designs inside of the panels. On the front of the trunk, transfer one panel, flip the pattern and transfer a mirrored image on the second panel.
4. Paint the Black areas outside the panels first, using a brush. Let dry.

PAINT THE DESIGN

Border:
Refer to the Borders Painting Worksheet.
1. Add the border lines around the panels with the 10/0 liner and Antique Gold.

2. Add small S-strokes with a #1 round and Antique Gold to make the rope border.

Scrolls:
Refer to the Scrolls Painting Worksheets.
1. Paint the scroll lines with Honey Brown.
2. Add the rounded tips to the scroll lines with Antique Gold.

Large Leaves Around Florals:
Refer to the Leaves Painting Worksheet.
1. Basecoat the larger leaves around the fruits and florals with a #4 filbert and Hauser Green Dark.
2. Add shorter strokes with Pine Green, then Avocado.
3. Highlight with a filbert rake and White.

Leaf Ferns:
Refer to the Leaves & Vines Painting Worksheet.
1. Paint the center stem with the 10/0 liner and Avocado.
2. Add small leaves on each side of the stem with the #2 filbert and Avocado.
3. Dot the berries with the #1 round and a mixture of Antique Gold + White.

Fruits:
1. Paint the apples, following the instructions on the *Apple Painting Worksheet.*
2. Paint the pears and plums, following the instructions on the *Pears & Plums Painting Worksheet.*

Roses:
Follow the instructions on the C-Stroke Rose Painting Worksheet, but change the palette.
1. Basecoat the roses with Burgundy.
2. Define the petals and cup of the rose with a pink mixture of Burgundy + White.
3. Highlight with White.
4. Tap in the center with Antique Gold.

Continued on page 75

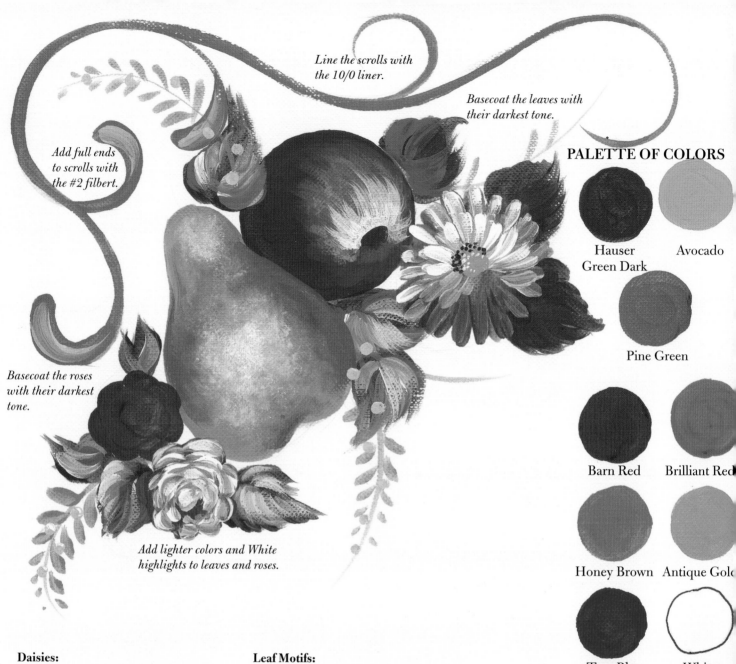

Line the scrolls with the 10/0 liner.

Basecoat the leaves with their darkest tone.

Add full ends to scrolls with the #2 filbert.

Basecoat the roses with their darkest tone.

Add lighter colors and White highlights to leaves and roses.

PALETTE OF COLORS

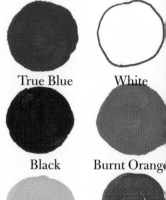

Hauser Green Dark

Avocado

Pine Green

Barn Red

Brilliant Red

Honey Brown

Antique Gold

True Blue

White

Black

Burnt Orange

Camel

Burgundy

Daisies:

Refer to the Daisies Painting Worksheet.

1. Paint the yellow daisies, following the instructions on the Painting Worksheet, but changing the palette to Antique Gold, Camel, White, and Barn Red.

2. Paint the peach daisies, following the same instructions, but changing the palette to Barn Red, Burnt Orange, and White.

3. Dot the daisy centers with the 10/0 liner, using Honey Brown and White.

Vines:

Follow the instructions on the Leaves & Vines Painting Worksheet, but change the palette.

1. Paint the vines with Avocado.

2. Add smaller leaves with Avocado and Pine Green.

Leaf Motifs:

Follow the instructions for Border #7 on the Borders Painting Worksheet.

Add leaf motifs on the Black areas around and between the panels as shown. Let dry.

FINISHING

1. Wipe the entire surface of the trunk with gel stain.

2. After a few minutes, wipe off the gel stain. Be sure to wipe with the grain of the wood. Use a small, old brush to smooth away any gel stain that has pooled in crevices or carved areas. Let dry.

3. Finish with two coats of water base polyurethane applied with a small cloth roller. Use a brush for detail areas. Let dry between coats. ❦

Closeup of Top

Closeup of front panel

Pattern

Panels
Enlarge @ 180%
for actual size

Pattern for Top
Enlarge @ 180%
for actual size

Connect at dotted lines
to complete pattern.

Part B

Part A

ROSE CAMEO TABLE

Simple yet elegant, this design could be used on almost any piece of furniture. The background of the oval panel is done here in black, but a cream or pale green would lighten the look of this classic design.

SUPPLIES

- Acrylic paints *(See Palette of Colors)*
- Extender medium
- Brushes
  Liner – 10/0
  Filbert – #2, #4, #6
  Filbert Rake – ⅛", ¼"
  Flat – 1"
  Round – #1, #2
- Rectangular gateleg or drop leaf table.
- Walnut gel stain
- Waterbase polyurethane
- Tools & supplies for preparing, transferring, antiquing, and finishing

PREPARATION

This was an older piece with minor flaws and damage. The finish was worn and there were a few small scratches.

1. Prepare furniture piece for painting. See "Preparing Stained and Sealed Wood" in the General Information chapter.
2. Trace and transfer the oval outline.
3. Paint the oval with a 1" flat brush and Black. Let dry.
4. Transfer the borders, scrolls and floral design.

PAINT THE DESIGN

Border:

Refer to the Borders Painting Worksheet.

1. Referring to Border #2, paint the teardrop stroke border around the Black oval with a #2 filbert and Golden Brown.
2. Add dots between strokes with Golden Brown.

Scrolls:

Refer to the Scrolls Painting Worksheets.

1. Paint scroll lines with Honey Brown.
2. Add the rounded tips to the scroll lines with Golden Brown.
3. Referring to Scroll IV, add leaves to the scrolls with Forest Moss and Pine Green.

Continued on page 80

Transfer and paint the Black oval first, then the scrolls, borders, and florals.

Paint the scroll lines with the 10/0 liner. Use the #2 filbert or #2 round to paint the scroll ends.

PALETTE OF COLORS

White

Black   Camel   Antique Rose   Forest Moss

Burgundy   Pine Green   Golden Brown   Honey Brown

...CONTINUED

Leaves Around Florals:

Refer to the Leaves Painting Worksheet.

1. Basecoat the leaves with the #4 filbert and Pine Green.
2. Stroke with Forest Moss, then Golden Brown.
3. Highlight with a filbert rake and White. Let dry.

Leaf Ferns:

Refer to the Leaves & Vines Painting Worksheet.

1. Paint the center stem with the 10/0 liner and Forest Moss.
2. Add small leaves on each side of the stem with the #2 filbert and Forest Moss, then Pine Green. Let dry.

Hydrangea Floral:

Follow the instructions on the Hydrangea Painting Worksheet, but change the palette.

1. Basecoat the hydrangea with Honey Brown.
2. Add petals with Camel.
3. Highlight petals with White.

Yellow Petal Filler Flowers:

Follow the instructions on the Bud Rose & Filler Flowers Painting Worksheet.

Large Roses:

Follow the instructions on the Filbert Rose Painting Worksheet, but change the palette.

1. Basecoat the large roses with Burgundy.
2. Define the petals and cup of the rose with Antique Rose.
3. Highlight with White.

Small Roses:

Follow the instructions on the C-Stroke Rose Painting Worksheet, but change the palette.

1. Basecoat the smaller roses with Honey Brown.
2. Define the petals and cup of the rose with Golden Brown.
3. Highlight with White.

Vines:

Follow the instructions on the Leaves & Vines Painting Worksheet, but change the palette.

1. Paint the vines with Forest Moss.
2. Add smaller leaves with Forest Moss and Pine Green.
3. Using the 10/0 liner, add tiny 4-dot flowers and 1-dot flowers randomly along the vine with White paint.

FINISHING

1. Wipe the entire surface of the table with gel stain.
2. After a few minutes, wipe off the gel stain. Be sure to wipe with the grain of the wood. Use a small, old brush to smooth away any gel stain that has pooled in crevices or carved areas. Let dry.
3. Finish with two coats of water base polyurethane applied with a small cloth roller. Use a brush for detail areas. Let dry between coats. ❧

Closeup of Front

Closeup of Top

Patterns

Enlarge @ 285% for actual size

Table Top

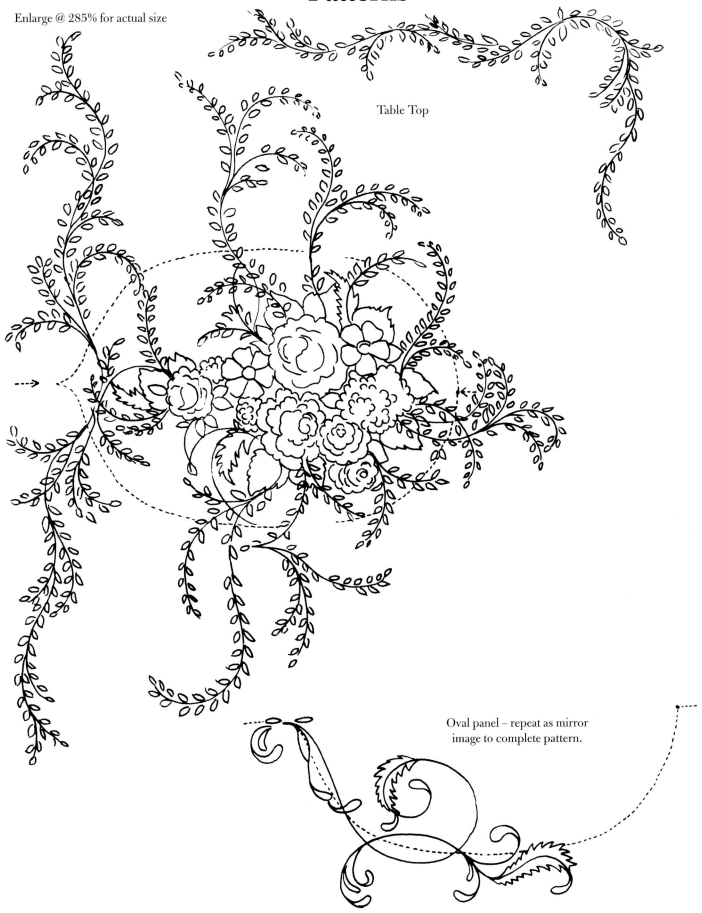

Oval panel – repeat as mirror
image to complete pattern.

HYDRANGEA RUSTIC BENCH

This is one of my favorite designs. We all love a garden, and you can enjoy this one all year long!

SUPPLIES

- Acrylic paints *(See Palette of Colors)*
- Extender medium
- Brushes
  Liner – 10/0
  Filbert – #2, #4, #6
  Filbert Rake – ⅛", ¼"
  Flat – #2, #4, 1"
  Round – #2
  Deerfoot – ¼"

- Wooden bench or stool
- Black latex paint
- Faux finish medium
- Container for mixing paint
- Walnut gel stain
- Waterbase polyurethane
- Tools & supplies for preparing, transferring, antiquing, and finishing

PALETTE OF COLORS

Deep Burgundy

Pine Green

Camel

Golden Brown

Baby Pink

True Red

Burnt Sienna

Forest Moss

Hauser Green Dark

Leaf Green

Antique White

White

Honey Brown

Burnt Umber

Baby Blue

True Blue

Purple

Black

PREPARATION

This bench was hand made from new, raw wood.

1. Dust the surface with an old large paint brush.
2. Fill and sand any rough areas, nail holes, or small cracks. Don't overdo it – you want a rustic look.
3. Mix one part Black latex paint to two parts faux finish medium in a container. With a large brush or rag, apply the mixture to the entire surface, following the grain. We are "staining" this piece to give it a worn look. Use a paint brush to feather out any blunt paint edges. Add a second coat if you want the color darker. Let dry.
4. Trace and transfer the design.

Basecoat leaves in the darkest green.

Add lighter green to leaves.

Use the #2 filbert rake for White highlights.

84

PAINT THE DESIGN

Flower Pots:
Refer to the Flower Pots Painting Worksheet.
Paint the three pots, following the instructions for the Terra Cotta Flower Pot. Vary shading and highlights to make each pot appear different.

Leaves Around Hydrangeas & Daisies:
Refer to the Leaves Painting Worksheet.
1. Basecoat the leaves with the #4 filbert and Hauser Green Dark.
2. Stroke with Forest Moss.
3. Highlight with a filbert rake and White. Let dry.

Geraniums:
Follow the instructions on the Geranium Painting Worksheet.

Hydrangeas:
Follow the instructions on the Hydrangea Painting Worksheet.

Daisies:
Follow the instructions on the Daisy Painting Worksheet, but change the palette.
1. Paint the daisy centers Honey Brown.
2. Paint the petals with Golden Brown, then Camel.
3. Highlight the petals with White.
4. Dot the daisy centers with Pine Green and White.

Vines:
Follow the instructions on the Leaves & Vines Painting Worksheet, but change the palette.
1. Paint the vines with Forest Moss.
2. Add smaller leaves with Forest Moss and Hauser Green Dark.

FINISHING
1. Distress the surface by sanding with medium sandpaper, sanding with the grain. Be gentle when sanding over your artwork; sand just enough to give it an aged look. Dust the sanded area well.
2. Wipe the entire surface of the bench with gel stain.
3. After a few minutes, wipe off the gel stain. Be sure to wipe with the grain of the wood. Use a small, old brush to smooth away any gel stain that has pooled in crevices or carved areas. Let dry.
4. Finish with two coats of water base polyurethane applied with a small cloth roller. Use a brush for detail areas. Let dry between coats. ❦

Patterns

Top of Bench – Part A
Connect at dotted lines
to complete pattern.

Part A

Vines for side of bench.
Connect at dotted lines
to complete pattern.

Vines for side of bench

Part B

Connect at dotted
lines to complete
pattern.

Top of Bench – Part B

ROSE GARLAND DRESSER

This is a quaint piece with a lovely antique look. The base painting here is black with red roses but it would also be beautiful in white with pink roses. If you have a bedside table or headboard, consider using parts of the pattern to make a set.

SUPPLIES

- Acrylic paints *(See Palette of Colors)*
- Extender medium
- Brushes
  Liner – 10/0
  Filbert – #2, #4
  Filbert Rake – ⅛"
  Flat – 1"
  Round – #2
- Chest of drawers
- Liquid sander
- Black latex paint, semi-gloss or satin
- Angled trim brush
- 2" paint pad
- Dark Walnut gel stain
- Waterbase polyurethane
- Tools & supplies for preparing, transferring, antiquing, and finishing

PREPARATION

This piece was painted black and just needed another coat of paint to refresh the finish.

1. Prepare furniture piece for painting. See "Preparing Stained and Sealed Wood" in the General Information chapter.
2. Apply black latex background paint with a small fabric roller and a good brush. Let dry.
3. Remove the drawers. Paint the front of the dresser with pale gold (one part Golden Brown to one part White) using a 2" paint pad. Also paint the beveled edge of the dresser top. Let dry. Replace the drawers.
4. Trace and transfer the design on each of the dresser drawers. Repeat the second drawer design on each drawer below, alternating with a flipped mirror image.

Continued on page 90

Camel

Golden Brown

White

Forest Moss

Hauser Green Dark

Baby Blue

Honey Brown

Lilac

Baby Pink

Brilliant Red

Basecoat leaves and roses with their darkest tones.

Add pink strokes to rose.

Add lighter colors to leaves.

Add White to highlight.

. . . CONTINUED

PAINT THE DESIGN

Gold Garland:

Paint the gold rounded garland with the #2 filbert and Golden Brown, using teardrop strokes.

Large Leaves Around Florals:

Refer to the Leaves Painting Worksheet.

1. Basecoat the leaves with the #4 filbert and Hauser Green Dark.
2. Stroke with Forest Moss, then Honey Brown.
3. Highlight with a filbert rake and White. Let dry.

Filler Flowers & Small Leaves:

Refer to the Bud Rose & Filler Flowers Painting Worksheet.

1. Paint the yellow petal filler flowers, following the instructions on the Painting Worksheet.
2. Paint the blue filler flowers, following the instructions on the Painting Worksheet, but changing the palette to Lilac, then Baby Blue, and White.
3. Add small teardrop leaves at the tips and around the edges of petals with the #2 filbert and Hauser Green Dark.

Roses:

Follow the instructions on the C-Stroke Rose Painting Worksheet, but use the #2 filbert and change the palette.

1. Basecoat the roses with the #2 filbert and Brilliant Red.
2. Define the petals and cup of the rose with Baby Pink.
3. Highlight with White.

Vines:

Follow the instructions on the Leaves & Vines Painting Worksheet, but change the palette.

1. Paint the vines with Hauser Green Dark.
2. Add smaller leaves with Hauser Green Dark and Forest Moss.

FINISHING

1. Wipe the entire surface of the dresser with gel stain.
2. After a few minutes, wipe off the gel stain. Use a small, old brush to smooth away any gel stain that has pooled in crevices or carved areas. Let dry.
3. Finish with two coats of water base polyurethane applied with a small cloth roller. Use a brush for detail areas. Let dry between coats. ❦

Closeup of Top

Patterns

Enlarge @ 200% for actual size

Top Drawers

Lower Drawers

Flip and transfer mirrored image
for lower drawer.

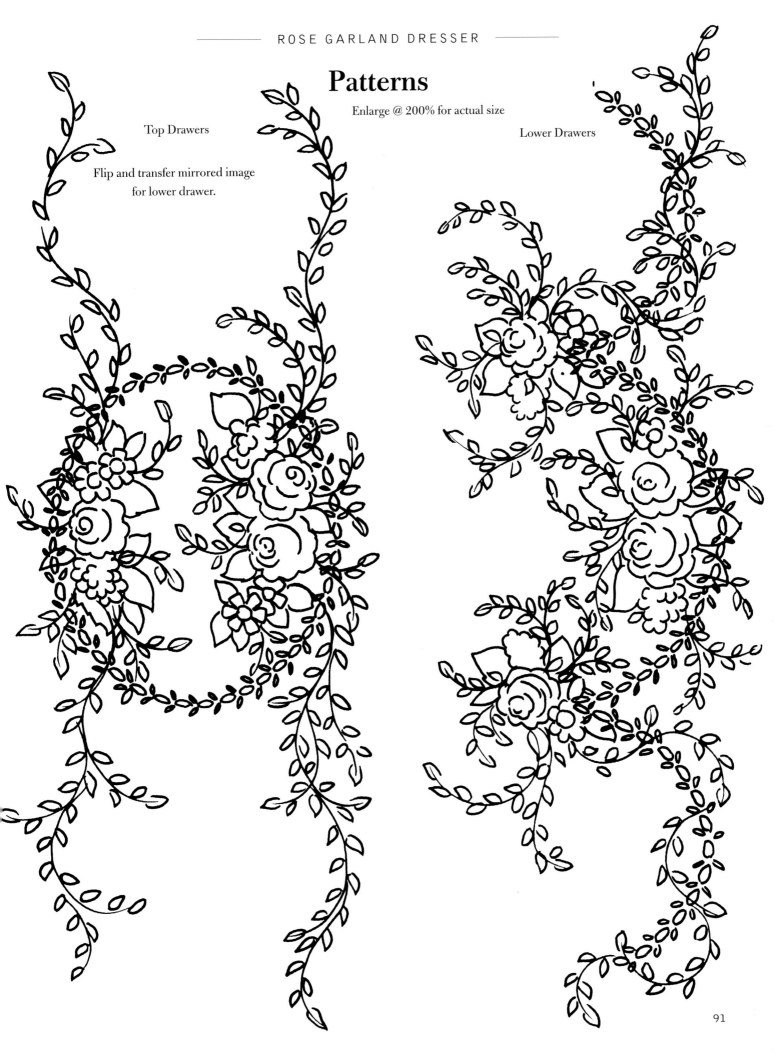

Use your compass to mark the bottom border.

Add crisscross lines, rope border, and dots.

Use a paint pad for the top border.

ROSE GARLAND LAMP

This lovely lamp will add warmth and beauty to any area of your home. The black background provides a wonderful contrast for the intricate florals and borders. This pattern would also be attractive on a white or cream background. You can always change the colors to match your decor.

PREPARATION

This lamp had minor flaws and damage. The tin shade was already painted black and in good condition.

1. Prepare lamp. See "Preparing Metal" in the General Information chapter.
2. Spray the lamp base and the shade with Black. Let dry.
3. Enlarge, trace and transfer the design on the shade and on the lamp.
4. Use your compass to make a line for the borders on the top and bottom of the shade.

Continued on page 94

PALETTE OF COLORS

Pine Green

Camel

Burnt Umber

Honey Brown

Olive Green

White

Golden Brown

SUPPLIES

- Acrylic paints *(See Palette of Colors)*
- Extender medium
- Brushes
  - Liner – 10/0
  - Filbert – #2, #4
  - Filbert Rake – ⅛", ¼"
  - Flat – 1"
  - Round – #1, #2
- Wooden lamp base and tin shade
- Black spray paint
- 2" paint pad
- Walnut gel stain
- Clear polyurethane spray
- Tools & supplies for preparing, transferring, antiquing, and finishing

...CONTINUED
PAINT THE DESIGN

Lamp Shade Borders:
Refer to the Borders Painting Worksheet.

1. Edge the top of the lamp shade with the 2" paint pad and Olive Green.
2. Add dots to the edge of the solid painted border with the #1 round and Olive Green.
3. Paint the crisscross design on the lower border of the lamp with the 10/0 liner and Olive Green.
4. Add the rope border and the dots inside the squares with the #1 round and Olive Green.

Lamp Base Borders:
Refer to the Borders Painting Worksheet.

1. Paint the solid band above the floral design using the 2" paint pad and Olive Green.
2. Paint a small border ring around the base of the lamp with Olive Green.
3. Add a rope border to the top of the 2" Olive Green band with the #1 round and Pine Green.
4. Add dots to the bottom of both Olive Green bands with the #1 round and Olive Green.

Lamp Shade Garland:
Paint garland leaves with teardrop strokes with a #2 filbert, using Pine Green, then Olive Green.

Leaves Around Florals:
Refer to the Leaves Painting Worksheet.

1. Basecoat the leaves with the #2 filbert and Pine Green.
2. Stroke with Olive Green, then a touch of Golden Brown.
3. Highlight with a filbert rake and White. Let dry.

Filler Flowers:
Follow the instructions on the Bud Rose & Filler Flowers Painting Worksheet, but change the palette.

1. Basecoat with Golden Brown.
2. Add petals with Camel.
3. Highlight with White.

Small Roses:
Follow the instructions on the C-Stroke Rose Painting Worksheet, but use the #2 filbert and change the palette.

1. Basecoat the smaller roses with the #2 filbert and Golden Brown.
2. Define the petals and cup of the rose with Camel.
3. Highlight with White.

Large Roses:
Follow the instructions on the C-Stroke Rose Painting Worksheet, but change the palette.

1. Basecoat the larger roses with Burnt Umber.
2. Define the petals and cup of the rose with Camel.
3. Highlight with White.

Vines:
Follow the instructions on the Leaves & Vines Painting Worksheet, but change the palette.

1. Paint the vines with Olive Green.
2. Add smaller leaves with Olive Green and Pine Green.
3. Add some vines and leaves to the foot of the lamp base.

FINISHING

1. Wipe the lamp and shade with gel stain.
2. After a few minutes, wipe off the gel stain. Use a small, old brush to smooth away any gel stain that has pooled in crevices or carved areas. Let dry.
3. Finish with two coats of clear polyurethane spray. Let dry between coats. ❦

Closeup of Base

Patterns

Enlarge @ 145% for actual size

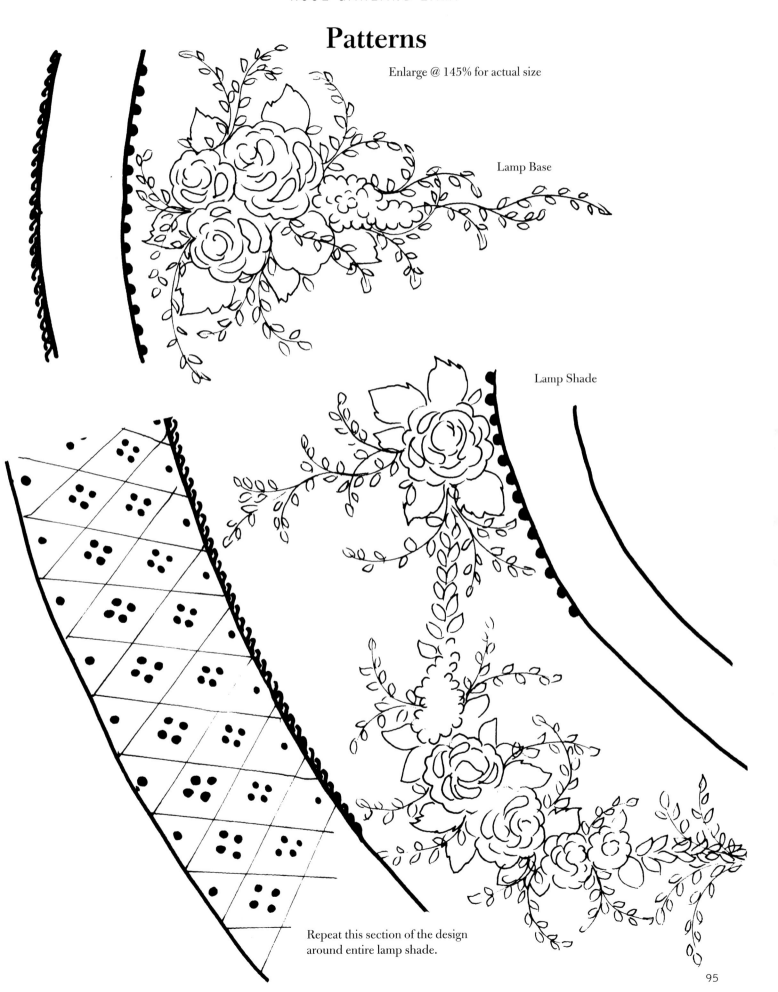

Lamp Base

Lamp Shade

Repeat this section of the design
around entire lamp shade.

Basecoat the leaves and roses with their darkest tones. Add lighter shades, following the contours

Start dark with the filler florals and add lighter tones.

Add lighter colors and White highlights.

PALETTE OF COLORS

Burnt Umber

Barn Red

Golden Brown

White

Pine Green

Olive Green

Dusty Rose

ROSE BOUQUET GATELEG TABLE

This heavenly garland is gorgeous, whether the table leaves are raised or lowered. It would be just as lovely on a solid oval tabletop.

SUPPLIES

- Acrylic paints *(See Palette of Colors)*
- Extender medium
- Brushes
  Liner – 10/0
  Filbert – #2, #4, #6
  Filbert Rake – ⅛", ¼"
  Round – #2
- Gateleg or drop leaf table
- Walnut gel stain
- Waterbase polyurethane
- Tools & supplies for preparing, transferring, antiquing, and finishing

PREPARATION

This was an older piece with minor flaws and damage. The finish was worn and there were a few small scratches.

1. Prepare furniture piece for painting. See "Preparing Stained and Sealed Wood" in the General Information chapter.
2. Enlarge, trace and transfer the design on the top and one leaf of the table. Flip the pattern and transfer a mirrored image on the other leaf of the table. Use portions of the pattern given to create a design for the entire table leaf and ends of top as pictured.

PAINT THE DESIGN

Large Leaves & Garlands:
Refer to the Leaves Painting Worksheet.

1. Basecoat the large leaves with the #4 filbert and Pine Green.

2. Stroke the large leaves with Olive Green, then Golden Brown.

3. Paint the garland with teardrop stroke leaves in the same colors.

4. Highlight with the ⅛" filbert rake and White. Let dry.

Filler Flowers:

Follow the instructions on the Bud Rose & Filler Flowers Painting Worksheet, but change the palette.

1. Basecoat with Burnt Umber.

2. Add petals with Golden Brown.

3. Highlight with White.

4. Paint the flower centers and dots.

Small Brown Roses:

Follow the instructions on the C-Stroke Rose Painting Worksheet, but change the palette.

1. Basecoat the brown roses with Burnt Umber.

2. Define the petals and cup of the rose with Golden Brown.

3. Highlight with White.

Small Red Roses:

Follow the instructions on the C-Stroke Rose Painting Worksheet, but change the palette.

1. Basecoat the red roses with Barn Red.

2. Define the petals and cup of the rose with Dusty Rose.

3. Highlight with White.

Large Brown Roses:

Follow the instructions on the Filbert Rose Painting Worksheet, but change the palette.

1. Basecoat the brown roses with Burnt Umber.

2. Define the petals and cup of the rose with Golden Brown.

3. Highlight with White.

Large Red Roses:

Follow the instructions on the Filbert Rose Painting Worksheet, but change the palette.

1. Basecoat the red roses with Barn Red.

2. Define the petals and cup of the rose with Dusty Rose.

3. Highlight with White.

Vines:

Follow the instructions on the Leaves & Vines Painting Worksheet, but change the palette.

1. Paint the vines with a thinned mixture of Olive Green + Golden Brown.

2. Add smaller leaves with Pine Green and a mixture of Olive Green + Golden Brown.

FINISHING

1. Wipe the entire surface of the table with gel stain.

2. After a few minutes, wipe off the gel stain. Be sure to wipe with the grain of the wood. Use a small, old brush to smooth away any gel stain that has pooled in crevices or carved areas. Let dry.

3. Finish with two coats of water base polyurethane applied with a small cloth roller. Use a brush for detail areas. Let dry between coats. ❦

Pattern

Use portions of this pattern to transfer to other areas of table to create a design covering the entire leaf.

Closeup of Top

98

Pattern

Pictured on Page 101.
Enlarge @ 145%
for actual size

SCROLLS & ROSES TRAY

Hand-painted trays are a favorite item for collectors. This tray is a perfect house-warming or hostess gift.

SUPPLIES

- Acrylic paints *(See Palette of Colors)*
- Extender medium
- Brushes
  Liner – 10/0
  Filbert – #2, #4, #6
  Filbert Rake – ⅛", ¼"
  Flat – 1"
  Round – #2
- Wooden tray
- Black spray paint, satin finish
- ½" paint pad
- Walnut gel stain
- Clear polyurethane spray
- Tools & supplies for preparing, transferring, antiquing, and finishing

PREPARATION

1. Prepare the tray. See "Preparing Stained and Sealed Wood" in the General Information chapter.
2. Spray with black paint. Wear your gloves and long sleeves. Work in a well-ventilated area. Let dry.
3. Trace and transfer the oval and scrolls.

PAINT THE DESIGN

Oval & Scrolls:
Refer to the Scrolls Painting Worksheet.

1. Paint the oval with the 1" flat and Sandstone. Let dry.
2. Paint the scrolls with Golden Brown. Let dry.
3. Add the rounded tips with Honey Brown. Let dry.
4. Transfer the florals and greenery on top of the painted oval.

Transfer and paint the oval first, then transfer and paint the scrolls, florals, and greenery.

PALETTE OF COLORS

Hauser Green Dark   White

 Golden Brown

 Honey Brown

 Sandstone

 Burgundy

 Peach

 Celery

Leaves Around Florals:

Refer to the Leaves Painting Worksheet.

1. Basecoat the leaves with the #4 filbert and Hauser Green Dark.
2. Stroke with Celery.
3. Highlight with a filbert rake and White. Let dry.

Filler Flowers:

Follow the instructions on the Bud Rose & Filler Flowers Painting Worksheet, but change the palette.

1. Basecoat with Honey Brown.
2. Add petals with Golden Brown.
3. Highlight with White.

Large Roses:

Follow the instructions on the Filbert Rose Painting Worksheet, but change the palette.

1. Basecoat the large roses with Burgundy.
2. Define the petals and cup of the rose with Peach.
3. Highlight with White.

Rosebuds:

1. Make teardrop strokes with a #2 filbert and Burgundy.
2. Add strokes of Peach to the rosebuds.
3. Highlight with small strokes of White.

Vines:

Follow the instructions on the Leaves & Vines Painting Worksheet, but change the palette.

1. Paint the vines with Celery.
2. Add smaller leaves to the vines with Celery, a mixture of Celery + Sandstone, and Hauser Green Dark.
3. Add small leaves to the bases of the rosebuds with the same brush and colors.

Border:

Refer to the Borders Painting Worksheet.

1. Paint the outside border of the tray with a ½" inch paint pad and Golden Brown. Let dry.
2. Add the small wavy border with the 10/0 liner and Celery. Let dry.

FINISHING

1. Wipe the entire surface of the tray with gel stain.
2. After a few minutes, wipe off the gel stain. Be sure to wipe with the grain of the wood. Use a small, old brush to smooth away any gel stain that has pooled in crevices or carved areas. Let dry.
3. Finish with two coats of clear polyurethane spray. Let dry between coats. ❦

Basecoat the leaves, roses, and florals in their darkest tones.

Add lighter C-stroke petals to the roses.

Add lighter colors and White to highlight.

WHITE ROSES CHEST

Muted tones on a parchment finish give the chest an understated yet elegant appeal.

SUPPLIES

- Acrylic paints *(See Palette of Colors)*
- Extender medium
- Brushes
  Liner – 10/0
  Filbert – #2, #4, #6
  Filbert Rake – ⅛", ¼"
  Round – #2
- Chest of drawers, unfinished wood
- White latex paint
- Taupe acrylic paint
- Faux finishing medium
- Sea sponge
- Waterbase polyurethane
- Tools & supplies for preparing, transferring, antiquing, and finishing

PREPARATION

1. Prepare chest. See "Preparing Unfinished Wood" in the General Information chapter.
2. Base paint the pieces with white latex paint.
3. Apply a parchment finish to surface. *See page 104 for Parchment Finish instructions.*
4. Trace and transfer the design to the chest. Add some vines and flowers to the bottom of the design to extend it onto lower drawers as shown in photo.

Continued on page 104

PALETTE OF COLORS

White

Pine Green   Celery   Burnt Umber   Black   Camel

...CONTINUED

PAINT THE DESIGN

Wreaths & Leaves:

Refer to the Leaves Painting Worksheet.

1. Basecoat the leaves surrounding the flowers with the #4 filbert and Pine Green. Stroke the wreath greenery with the same brush and color.
2. Stroke the leaves and wreath greenery with Celery.
3. Highlight with White.

Filler Flowers:

Follow the instructions on the Bud Rose & Filler Flowers Painting Worksheet, but change the palette.

1. Basecoat with Burnt Umber.
2. Add petals with Camel.
3. Highlight with White.

Small Roses:

Follow the instructions on the C-Stroke Rose Painting Worksheet, but change the palette.

1. Basecoat the smaller roses with Black.

2. Define the petals and cup of the rose with Burnt Umber.
3. Highlight with White.

Large Roses:

Follow the instructions on the Filbert Rose Painting Worksheet, but change the palette.

1. Basecoat the large roses with Black.
2. Define the petals and cup of the rose with Burnt Umber and Camel.
3. Highlight with White.

Vines:

Follow the instructions on the Leaves & Vines Painting Worksheet, but change the palette.

1. Paint the vines with Pine Green.
2. Add smaller leaves with Pine Green and Celery.

FINISHING

Finish with two coats of water base polyurethane applied with a small cloth roller. Use a brush for detail areas. Let dry between coats. ❧

Parchment Finish:

1. Mix one part Taupe acrylic paint with one part faux finish medium. Use the sponge to wipe the entire chest with the mixture.
2. Working quickly while the mixture is wet, squeeze excess paint from the sponge and tap it lightly in a random pattern on the surface, picking up paint. Continue squeezing out excess paint as you go. Let dry.

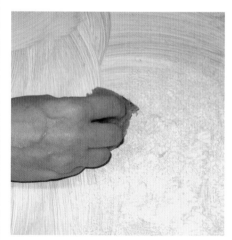

Patterns

Enlarge @ 200% for actual size

Extend vines and flowers at bottom, using photo as guide.

FRUIT CARTOUCHE ARMOIRE

Everyone loves red! The harmonious arrangement of fruits and flowers makes a dramatic statement on this lovely piece.

SUPPLIES

- Acrylic paints *(See Palette of Colors)*
- Extender medium
- Brushes
  - Liner – 10/0
  - Filbert – #2, #4, #6
  - Filbert Rake – ⅛", ¼"
  - Flat – 1"
  - Round – #2
  - Angle – #2
  - Deerfoot – ¼"
- Double door cabinet or armoire
- Salmon latex paint
- 2" paint pad
- Walnut gel stain
- Waterbase polyurethane
- Tools & supplies for preparing, transferring, antiquing, and finishing

PREPARATION

1. Prepare piece for painting. See "Preparing Stained and Sealed Wood" in the General Information chapter.
2. Paint the piece with salmon latex paint. Let dry.
3. Paint the wide borders around each panel with a 2" paint pad and Barn Red. Let dry.
4. Add the small straight line on the edge of the red border with a pale gold mixture of Golden Brown + White, using a #2 angle brush turned on its side. Let dry.
5. The designs on these doors were done a little differently than most of the patterns. Use the patterns given to either cut card-stock templates or to transfer the elements in the arrangement of your choice. If you cut the cardstock templates, you can cut as many shapes as needed, then tape them to doors until you have the arrangement you like. Then you can trace around the shapes to aid in painting.

PAINT THE DESIGN

Large Leaves:

Refer to the Leaves Painting Worksheet.

1. Basecoat the large leaves surrounding the fruits and flowers with the #4 filbert and Hauser Green Dark.

Continued on next page

Basecoat leaves with their darkest tone.

Use the #2 filbert rake to add veins to leaves.

Use the deerfoot to blend golds and browns in the pear.

PALETTE OF COLORS

Camel

White

Golden Brown

Burnt Sienna

Barn Red

Deep Burgundy

Hauser Green Dark

Celery

...CONTINUED

2. Stroke with Celery, then Golden Brown.
3. Highlight with a filbert rake and White. Let dry.

Pears:

Follow the instructions on the Pears & Plums Painting Worksheet, but change the palette.

1. Basecoat the pears with Golden Brown.
2. Shade the edges with Burnt Sienna.
3. Blend Camel on the center of the pear.
4. Highlight with White.

Peaches:

Peaches are painted like plums, but larger. Follow the Plum instructions on the Pears & Plums Painting Worksheet, but use a #6 filbert and change the palette.

1. Basecoat the peaches with Golden Brown.
2. Shade the edges with Barn Red.
3. Make the C-stroke with Camel. Blend Camel with the deerfoot.
4. Highlight with White.

Cherries:

1. Basecoat the cherries with a #4 filbert and Deep Burgundy.
2. With the ¼" deerfoot, tap in Barn Red, then White, blending as you go.
3. Highlight with the #4 filbert and White.

Daisies:

Follow the instructions on the Daisy Painting Worksheet, but change the palette.

1. Paint the petals with Barn Red, then a mixture of Barn Red + White.
2. Highlight the petals with White.
3. Paint the centers as shown on worksheet.

Small Roses:

Follow the instructions on the C-Stroke Rose Painting Worksheet, but change the palette.

1. Basecoat the smaller roses with Deep Burgundy.
2. Define the petals and cup of the rose with Barn Red.
3. Highlight with White.
4. Tap Golden Brown in the center of the rose.

Large Roses:

Follow the instructions on the Filbert Rose Painting Worksheet, but change the palette.

1. Basecoat the large roses with Deep Burgundy.
2. Define the petals and cup of the rose with Barn Red.
3. Highlight with White.
4. Tap small strokes of Golden Brown in the center of the rose.

Vines:

Follow the instructions on the Leaves & Vines Painting Worksheet, but change the palette.

1. Paint the vines with Celery.
2. Add smaller leaves with Celery and Hauser Green Dark. Let dry.

FINISHING

1. Wipe the entire surface of the piece with gel stain.
2. After a few minutes, wipe off the gel stain. Be sure to wipe with the grain of the wood. Use a small, old brush to smooth away any gel stain that has pooled in crevices or carved areas. Let dry.
3. Finish with two coats of water base polyurethane applied with a small cloth roller. Use a brush for detail areas. Let dry between coats. ❧

Patterns

Enlarge @ 145%
for actual size

Template Patterns –
cut out and arrange
as desired.

Use photo as a guide
for placement

ELEGANT SIDE TABLE

Less is More! This piece combines scrollwork and floral designs created with simple brush strokes – a great beginner project. Black is so stylish in today's home décor, this piece fits right in.

SUPPLIES

- Acrylic paints *(See Palette of Colors)*
- Extender medium
- Brushes
  Liner – 10/0
  Filbert – #2, #4, #6
  Filbert Rake – ⅛", ¼"
  Round – #2

- Oval wooden table
- Black latex paint
- Walnut gel stain
- Water base polyurethane
- Tools & supplies for preparing, transferring, antiquing, and finishing

PREPARATION

1. Prepare the table. See "Preparing Stained and Sealed Wood" in the General Information chapter.
2. Paint with black latex paint. Let dry.
3. Trace and transfer the design on one side of the tabletop. Flip and transfer a mirror image on the other side.

PAINT THE DESIGN

Scrolls:
Refer to the Scrolls Painting Worksheet.
1. Paint the scrolls with Honey Brown. Let dry.
2. Add the rounded tips to the scroll lines with Antique Gold. Let dry.

Continued on page 112

Basecoat leaves and roses with their darkest tones.

Add lighter colors and highlights.

PALETTE OF COLORS

Camel

White

Peach

Celery

Barn Red

Antique Gold

Hauser Green Dark

Olive Green

Honey Brown

110

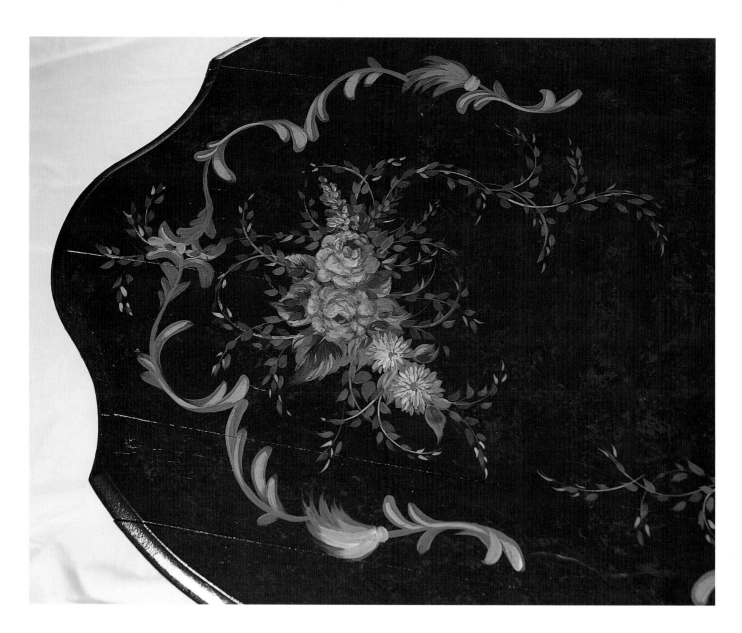

Leaves Around Florals:

Refer to the Leaves Painting Worksheet.

1. Basecoat the leaves with the #4 filbert and Hauser Green Dark.
2. Stroke with Olive Green, then Celery.
3. Highlight with a filbert rake and White. Let dry.

Daisies:

Follow the instructions on the Daisy Painting Worksheet.

Dot daisy centers with Hauser Green Dark, Barn Red, and White.

Filler Flowers:

Follow the instructions on the Bud Rose & Filler Flowers Painting Worksheet, but

change the palette.

1. Basecoat with Barn Red.
2. Add petals with Peach.
3. Highlight with White.

Large Roses:

Follow the instructions on the Filbert Rose Painting Worksheet, but change the palette.

1. Basecoat the large roses with Barn Red.
2. Define the petals and cup of the rose with Peach.
3. Highlight with White.

Vines:

Follow the instructions on the Leaves & Vines Painting Worksheet, but change the palette.

1. Paint the vines with Olive Green.

2. Add smaller leaves with Olive Green and Celery.

FINISHING

1. Wipe the entire surface of the piece with gel stain.
2. After a few minutes, wipe off the gel stain. Be sure to wipe with the grain of the wood. Use a small, old brush to smooth away any gel stain that has pooled in crevices or carved areas. Let dry.
3. Finish with two coats of water base polyurethane applied with a small cloth roller. Use a brush for detail areas. Let dry between coats. ❦

Pattern

Enlarge @ 170% for actual size

Repeat as mirror image
for opposite side.

FLORAL BOUQUET WINDOW

Glass windows are perfect for your decorative painting because they already have a frame. They can be hung indoors or outdoors and are charming on a patio or screened porch. Hang this painted window anywhere you'd like a lovely view!

PATTERN ON PAGE 119

SUPPLIES

- Acrylic paints (*See Palette of Colors*)
- Extender medium
- Brushes
  Liner – 10/0
  Filbert – #2, #4, #6
  Filbert Rake – ⅛", ¼"
  Flat – 1"
- Round – #2
  Deerfoot – ¼"
- Single-pane, wood-framed window
- Clear spray polyurethane
- 2" paint pad
- Tools & supplies for preparing and transferring

PREPARATION

1. Prepare window. See "Preparing Glass" in the General Information chapter.
2. Spray the surface of the glass lightly with clear polyurethane. This will make the glass cloudy. It gives the glass surface tooth so the acrylic paint will adhere. If the clear spray gets on the wood frame, don't worry. You will spray the entire window with the same clear polyurethane in the finishing step.
3. Instead of transferring the pattern, tape it to the back of the glass.

PAINT THE DESIGN

Borders:
Refer to the Borders Painting Worksheet.
1. Use a 2" paint pad and Burnt Umber to paint the wide border around the edges of the window.
2. Add dots to the inner edges of the border with the #2 filbert and Burnt Umber. Let dry.
3. Add the C-stroke border, following the instructions for Border #8.

Scrolls:
Refer to the Scrolls Painting Worksheet.
1. Paint the scroll lines with Honey Brown. Let dry.
2. Add the rounded tips to the scroll lines with Antique Gold. Let dry.

Vase:
1. Paint the container with the #4 filbert and Burnt Umber.

Basecoat florals in their darkest tones.

Add lighter colors and White.

Use a filbert rake to highlight leaves.

PALETTE OF COLORS

Antique Gold

Baby Blue

Alizarin Crimson

Orange

True Blue

Honey Brown

White

Pine Green

Olive Green

Burnt Umber

2. Highlight with the ⅛" filbert rake and Antique Gold, then White.

Leaves Around Flowers & Garland:
Refer to the Leaves Painting Worksheet.
1. Basecoat the leaves with the #4 filbert and Pine Green.
2. Stroke with Olive Green.
3. Highlight with a filbert rake and White. Let dry.

Filler Flowers:
Follow the instructions on the Bud Rose & Filler Flowers Painting Worksheet.

Small Roses:
Follow the instructions on the C-Stroke Rose Painting Worksheet, but change the palette.
1. Basecoat the smaller roses with Honey Brown.
2. Define the petals and cup of the rose with Antique Gold.
3. Highlight with White.

Tulips:
1. Using a #6 filbert, make large teardrop strokes with Orange, pulling down toward the center bottom of the flower.
2. Starting with the tallest center petal, create individual petals by pulling down with White.
3. To create more petals, make White C-strokes facing each other.
4. Add more White to the top edges of the petals.

Large Roses:
Follow the instructions on the Filbert Rose Painting Worksheet, but change the palette.
1. Basecoat the large roses with Alizarin Crimson.
2. Define the petals and cup of the rose with a mixture of Alizarin Crimson + White.
3. Highlight with White.

Vines:
Follow the instructions on the Leaves & Vines Painting Worksheet, but change the palette.
1. Paint the vines with Olive Green.
2. Add smaller leaves with Olive Green and Pine Green.

FINISHING
1. After the paint is completely dry, dust the window with your large brush.
2. Finish with two coats of clear spray polyurethane to seal the glass and wood surfaces. Let dry completely between coats. ❦

GARLAND & SCROLLS WINDOW

This elegant design could be used on many different pieces with a large flat surface. It would be beautiful painted on a large tray.

SUPPLIES

- Acrylic paints *(See Palette of Colors)*
- Extender medium
- Brushes
  Liner – 10/0
  Filbert – #2, #4, #6
  Filbert Rake – ⅛", ¼"
  Round – #2

- Single-pane, wood-framed window
- Clear spray polyurethane
- 2" paint pad
- Tools & supplies for preparing and transferring

PREPARATION

1. Prepare window. See "Preparing Glass" in the General Information chapter.
2. Spray the surface of the glass lightly with clear polyurethane. This will make the glass cloudy. It gives the glass surface tooth so the acrylic paint will adhere. If the clear spray gets on the wood frame, don't worry. You will spray the entire window with the same clear polyurethane in the finishing step.
3. Instead of transferring the pattern, tape it to the back of the glass.

PAINT THE DESIGN

Borders:
Refer to the Borders Painting Worksheet.
1. Use a 2" paint pad and Honey Brown to paint the wide border around the edges of the window.

PALETTE OF COLORS

Baby Pink

White

Peony Pink

True Blue

True Red

Purple

Honey Brown

Forest Moss

Pine Green

Use Honey Brown leaf strokes for ferns.

Basecoat the flower in Purple and True Blue.

Add highlights and flower center.

2. Add dots to the inner edges of the border with the #2 filbert and Honey Brown. Let dry.

3. Add the wavy border, following the instructions for Border #3 but using Pine Green.

Scrolls:

Refer to the Scrolls Painting Worksheet.

1. Paint the scroll lines with Honey Brown. Let dry.

2. Add the rounded tips to the scroll lines with Honey Brown. Let dry.

3. Add the leaf swag to the scrolls with teardrop strokes of the #2 filbert or round and Pine Green, then Forest Moss.

Container & Ribbon:

1. Paint the container with the #4 filbert and Honey Brown.

2. Highlight with the ⅛" filbert rake, using Honey Brown and White.

3. Paint the ribbon with a #2 round, using Honey Brown and White.

Leaves Around Florals:

Refer to the Leaves Painting Worksheet.

1. Basecoat the leaves surrounding the flowers in the container with the #4 filbert and Pine Green.

2. Stroke with Forest Moss.

3. Highlight with a filbert rake and White. Let dry.

Leaf Ferns:

Refer to the Leaves & Vines Painting Worksheet.

1. Paint the center stem with the 10/0 liner and Honey Brown.

2. Add small leaves on each side of the stem with the #4 filbert, using Honey Brown and a mixture of Honey Brown + White.

Bud Rose:

Follow the instructions on the Bud Rose & Filler Flowers Painting Worksheet.

Large Roses:

Follow the instructions on the Filbert Rose Painting Worksheet, but change the palette.

1. Basecoat the large roses with True Red.

2. Define the petals and cup of the rose with Peony Pink and Baby Pink.

3. Highlight with White.

Petal Filler Flowers:

Follow the instructions on the Bud Rose & Filler Flowers Painting Worksheet, but change the palette.

1. Using a #4 filbert, make each petal with facing C-strokes, one Purple and one True Blue.

2. Highlight petals with White.

3. Add small strokes with the ⅛" filbert rake and Honey Brown to the base of the petals.

4. Add the center to the flower with the #2 round and Honey Brown.

5. Add dots in the center of the flower with the #1 round, using Pine Green and White.

Vines:

Follow the instructions on the Leaves & Vines Painting Worksheet, but change the palette.

1. Paint the vines with Forest Moss.

2. Add smaller leaves with Forest Moss and Pine Green.

FINISHING

1. After the paint is completely dry, dust the window with your large brush.

2. Finish with two coats of clear spray polyurethane to seal the glass and wood surfaces. Let dry completely between coats. ❦

Pattern

Half Pattern – flip to repeat

Vase

Scroll
Actual size

Top
Enlarge @ 200% for actual size

Border (actual size)

Continue around window.

Pattern

Pictured on Page 115.
Enlarge @ 200% for actual size

Border – continue around

VICTORIAN SCROLLS & ROSES MIRROR

This design combines scrolls and simple floral designs to create an impressive statement in an entryway or formal dining room.

SUPPLIES

- Acrylic paints *(See Palette of Colors)*
- Extender medium
- Brushes
  Liner – 10/0
  Filbert – #2, #4, #6
  Filbert Rake – ⅛", ¼"
  Flat – 1"
  Round – #2
- Large, wood-framed mirror
- Paint pads – 2", 1"
- Walnut gel stain
- Waterbase polyurethane
- Tools & supplies for preparing, transferring, antiquing, and finishing

PREPARATION

1. Prepare the frame. See "Preparing Stained and Sealed Wood" in the General Information chapter.
2. Paint the top center panel solid Dark Chocolate with the 2" paint pad. Let dry.
3. Paint the outside solid border areas first, using a 1" paint pad and Dark Chocolate.
4. Place painter's tape to mask off square blocks at top and bottom of the frame. Paint inside the taped areas with the 1" flat and Dark Chocolate.
5. Trace and transfer the design on each area of the frame except the top center panel. On the top center panel, flip and transfer to make the mirrored image and complete the symmetrical design.

PAINT THE DESIGN

Scrolls:
Refer to the Scrolls Painting Worksheet.
1. Paint the scroll lines with Golden Brown. Let dry.
2. Add the rounded tips and flourishes to the scroll lines with a mixture of Golden Brown + Camel. Let dry.

Leaves Around Florals:
Refer to the Leaves Painting Worksheet.
1. Basecoat the leaves with the #4 filbert and Black Green.
2. Stroke with Avocado, then Camel.
3. Highlight with a filbert rake and White. Let dry.

Continued on page 122

PALETTE OF COLORS

Mauve   Barn Red   Golden Brown   Camel

White   Dark Chocolate   Avocado   Black Green

Add highlights to leaves with the filbert rake.

Use a #2 filbert or round. Pull to stem, shortening strokes as you approach the tip.

...CONTINUED

Closeup

Filler Flowers:

Follow the instructions on the Bud Rose & Filler Flowers Painting Worksheet, but change the palette.

1. Basecoat with Mauve.
2. Add petals with Camel.
3. Highlight with White.

Small Roses:

Follow the instructions on the C-Stroke Rose Painting Worksheet, but change the palette.

1. Basecoat the smaller roses with Dark Chocolate.
2. Define the petals and cup of the rose with Golden Brown.
3. Highlight with White.

Large Roses:

Follow the instructions on the Filbert Rose Painting Worksheet, but change the palette.

1. Basecoat the large roses with Barn Red.
2. Define the petals and cup of the rose with Mauve and Camel.
3. Highlight with White.

Vines:

Follow the instructions on the Leaves & Vines Painting Worksheet, but change the palette.

1. Paint the vines with Avocado.
2. Add smaller leaves with Black Green and Avocado.

Detail Borders:

Refer to the Borders Painting Worksheet.

1. Add detail borders on the brown borders as pictured, using a 10/0 liner and Camel for straight lines.
2. Continue with the liner and Camel, pulling strokes in toward the stem and shortening the strokes as you approach the tip.
3. Add dots with the #2 round.

FINISHING

1. Wipe the entire surface of the piece with gel stain.
2. After a few minutes, wipe off the gel stain. Be sure to wipe with the grain of the wood. Use a small, old brush to smooth away any gel stain that has pooled in crevices or carved areas. Let dry.
3. Finish with two coats of water base polyurethane applied with a small cloth roller. Use a brush for detail areas. Let dry between coats.
4. Install the mirror. ✿

Patterns

Enlarge @ 225% for actual size

Repeat as mirror image to complete design

Middle
Repeat from center as mirror
image to complete pattern.

Top

Leaf motif

Bottom

HOLD EVERYTHING TUB

This old galvanized washtub was a true find. It has a variety of uses indoors or out - icing down cold drinks, storing children's toys, or holding gardening supplies.

SUPPLIES

- Acrylic paints *(See Palette of Colors)*
- Extender medium
- Brushes
  Liner – 10/0

- Filbert – #2, #4, #6
- Filbert Rake – ⅛", ¼"
- Flat – 1"
- Round – #2
- Deerfoot – ¼"

- Large galvanized wash tub
- Walnut gel stain
- Waterbase polyurethane
- Tools & supplies for preparing, transferring, antiquing, and finishing

Basecoat the geranium in dark and medium reds.

Add pink and White to highlight the geranium.

PALETTE OF COLORS

Pine Green

Antique White   Purple

White   Golden Brown

Burnt Sienna   True Blue   Baby Blue

Baby Pink   Burgundy   True Red

Hauser
Green Dark   Leaf Green   Burnt Umber   Camel

124

PREPARATION

1. Prepare tub for painting. See "Preparing Metal" in the General Information chapter.
2. Trace and transfer the design.

PAINT THE DESIGN

Flower Pots:

Refer to the Flower Pots Painting Worksheet.

1. Paint the two terra cotta pots, following the instructions on the Painting Worksheet. Vary shading and highlights to make each pot appear different.
2. Paint the flow blue pot, following the instructions on the Painting Worksheet.

Leaves Around Hydrangeas:

Refer to the Leaves Painting Worksheet.

1. Basecoat the leaves with the #4 filbert and Hauser Green Dark.
2. Stroke with Leaf Green.
3. Highlight with White. Let dry.

Geraniums & Leaves:

Follow the instructions on the Geraniums Painting Worksheet.

Hydrangeas:

Follow the instructions on the Hydrangeas Painting Worksheet.

Long Leaf Ferns:

Refer to the Leaves & Vines Painting Worksheet.

1. Paint the center stem with a mixture of Hauser Green Dark + White.
2. Add leaves with a mixture of Hauser Green Dark + White, and White.

Vines:

Follow the instructions on the Leaves & Vines Painting Worksheet, but change the palette.

1. Paint the vines with Hauser Green Dark.
2. Add smaller leaves with a mixture of Leaf Green + White, and Hauser Green Dark.

FINISHING

1. Wipe the entire surface of the tub, inside and out, with gel stain.
2. After a few minutes, wipe off the gel stain. Let dry.
3. Finish with two coats of water base polyurethane applied with a small cloth roller. Use a brush for detail areas. Let dry between coats. ❧

Pattern

Part A

Enlarge @ 200% for
actual size

Connect at dotted lines
to complete pattern.

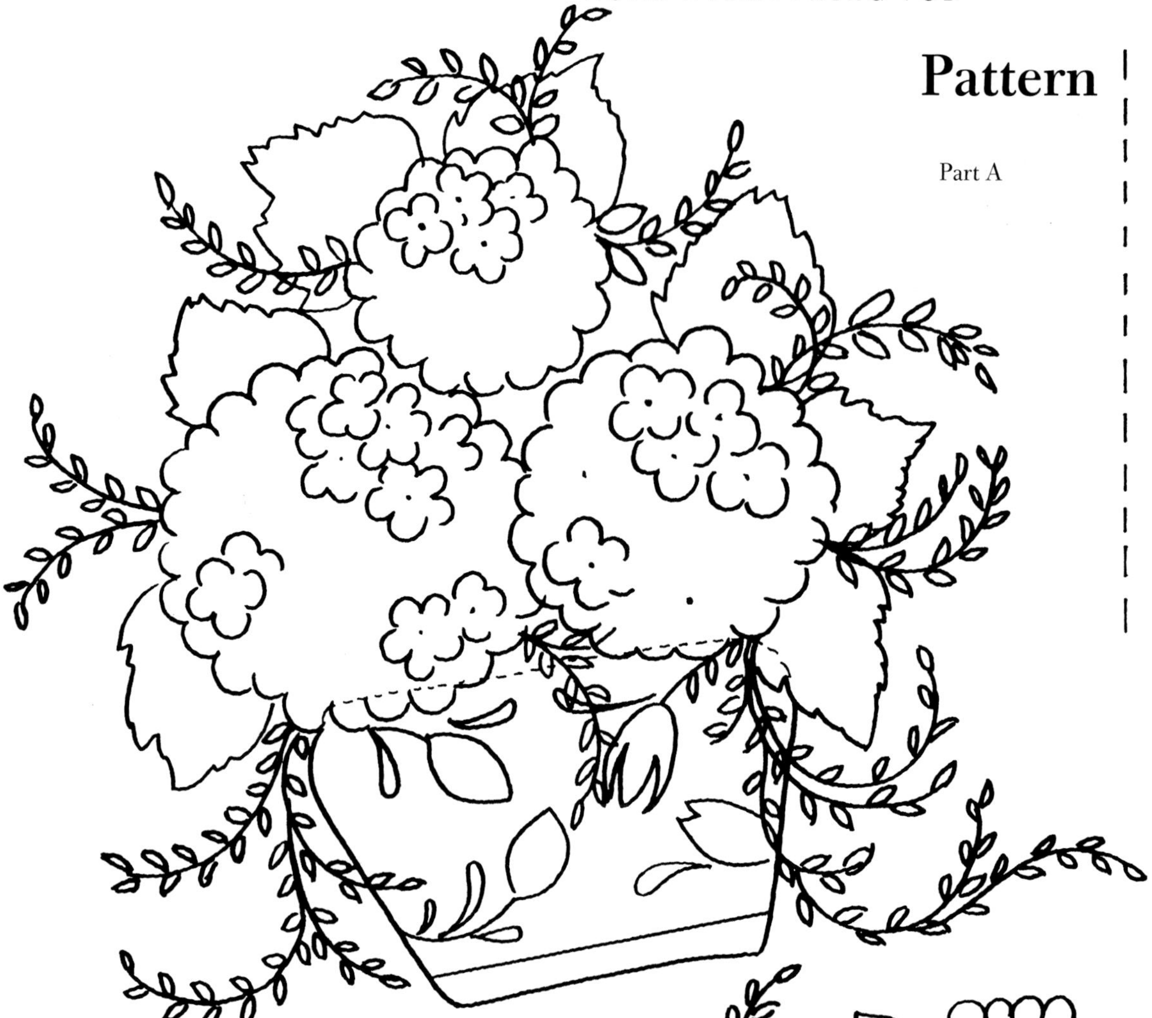

Part B

METRIC CONVERSION CHART

Inches to Millimeters and Centimeters

Inches	MM	CM	Inches	MM	CM
1/8	3	.3	2	51	5.1
1/4	6	.6	3	76	7.6
3/8	10	1.0	4	102	10.2
1/2	13	1.3	5	127	12.7
5/8	16	1.6	6	152	15.2
3/4	19	1.9	7	178	17.8
7/8	22	2.2	8	203	20.3
1	25	2.5	9	229	22.9
1-1/4	32	3.2	10	254	25.4
1-1/2	38	3.8	11	279	27.9
1-3/4	44	4.4	12	305	30.5

Yards to Meters

Yards	Meters	Yards	Meters
1/8	.11	3	2.74
1/4	.23	4	3.66
3/8	.34	5	4.57
1/2	.46	6	5.49
5/8	.57	7	6.40
3/4	.69	8	7.32
7/8	.80	9	8.23
1	.91	10	9.14
2	1.83		

INDEX

Continued on next page

INDEX